More Thematic Units
For
Creating The
Integrated Curriculum

A Companion Volume to

The Complete Guide To Thematic Units:

Creating The Integrated Curriculum

More Thematic Units
For
Creating The
Integrated Curriculum

A Companion Volume to

The Complete Guide To Thematic Units:

Creating The Integrated Curriculum

Liz Rothlein

Anthony D. Fredericks

Anita Meyer Meinbach

Christopher-Gordon Publishers, Inc.

Norwood, MA

Christopher-Gordon Publishers, Inc.
480 Washington Street
Norwood, MA 02062

Printed in the United States of America
10 9 8 7 6 5 4 3 2 1   99 98 97 96 95 94 93

ISBN: 926842-53-6

Dedication

To Harry Forgan, my colleague, friend, and mentor

who assisted me in launching my publishing career.

L.R.

To Susan Savia for sharing laughter and enriching life.

A.D.F.

To Suzy and Andrew may you always cherish knowledge and discovery.

A.M.M.

Introduction

Welcome to wonder! Welcome to possibilities! Welcome to the creative spirit and delightful curiosity of kids! Welcome to the *literature-rich* classroom!

Our experiences as classroom teachers and reading specialists has taught us that *kids + books* is the most magical combination in any elementary classroom. Sharing a voyage of discovery, a tale well told, a book twice told, a story of mystery, or a legend of long ago stimulates the senses and takes learners on imaginative journeys of "what-if's" and "did you know's?" Literature provides children with a vehicle that can tour any dimension of the human mind.

When teachers meld quality children's literature with practical and meaningful learning opportunities, then students can explore and appreciate any form of knowledge—both real and imaginary. **Thematic units** encourage students to become active participants in the learning process. Additionally, they offer teachers innumerable opportunities to assist their students in reaching for all the possibilities books hold.

In our previous book—*The Complete Guide to Thematic Units: Creating the Integrated Curriculum*—we wrote about the design and use of thematic units and included eight complete units for immediate classroom use. This book is an extension of that earlier volume. In the following pages we present eight more units for your classroom. We invite you to obtain a copy of the initial book so that you may have the structures and outlines necessary for the successful use of thematic units in your classroom. This book certainly stands on its own, but its utility will be considerably enhanced if it is used in combination with the whole language ideas, teaching suggestions, practical strategies, and success-oriented techniques delineated in the first volume.

We sincerely hope you enjoy sharing these units with your students. We know your classroom will be filled with all the joy and incredible possibilities a literature-rich curriculum can bring. We also know your students will be presented with a cornucopia of learning opportunities and literacy ventures that is possible through thematic instruction.

Welcome to wonder!

Liz Rothlein
Anthony D. Fredericks
Anita M. Meinbach

Contents

PART I:

The Value of Thematic Units

The piercing cries of macaws, parrots, and toucans filled the air with a cacophony of sounds. Insects of every dimension, size, and shape could be heard buzzing and whirring through the air and scraping across the weather-hewn bark of trees. The melodious gurgling of a nearby stream mixed with animal sounds to create an orchestral mix of basses and trebles that ebbed and flowed across the landscape.

High overhead, scores of liana vines hung in a dozen different places. The entire area was filled with splashes of green and dotted with a palette of iridescent colors. Occasionally the air was filled with the whir of wings and the echoes of distant monkeys. An occasional roar or soft-bellied slithering could be heard, and it soon became evident that this was a place filled with a diversity of life—both seen and unseen.

Visitors entering Jerri Villard's third grade classroom often feel as though they have been transported to some verdant Amazonian forest. Jerri's room is less a classroom and more an ecological wonderland awash in magnificent sights and sounds. She and her students have worked hard to transform their room into a rain forest ecosystem that is so close to the original that one might expect a stealthy jaguar to creep out of the shadows or a giant python to coil itself around the leg of a desk.

Jerri has been a third grade teacher in central Kansas for the past six years. She is fully aware that most of her students may never have the opportunity to travel to Brazil, The Cameroons, Costa Rica, or any other rain forest country to experience the sounds and sights of this endangered environment. So, too, does she realize that the rain forests of the world are on the brink of elimination and that the next generation of kids must work together to help preserve the plant and animal species that live in this fragile ecosystem.

In order to actively involve her students in a host of positive learning experiences, Jerri set out to create a thematic unit on "Rain Forests." Jerri engaged her students in the creation and development of a plethora of integrated activities (see our previous book—*The Complete Guide to Thematic Units: Creating the Integrated Curriculum*). By offering her students active opportunities to become involved in the design of the thematic unit, Jerri was able to provide authentic projects that gave her students a sense of responsibility for their own learning and a feeling of "ownership" in the activities selected, pursued, and completed.

Let's take a few moments and look in on Jerri's class as her students explore some of the mysteries and marvels of rain forest life:

Dappled sunlight bounced across the walls of Jerri's classroom as students filled the air with the excitement of new discoveries and the enthusiasm of active learning. A small group of three girls was putting the finishing touches on a hand-made terrarium they had constructed from plastic soda bottles—soil, pebbles, charcoal, and an array of small plants lay scattered across one of the science tables. The terrarium (one of several) was to be set up on the window sill and the growth of its life forms tracked and recorded over a period of several weeks.

Joshua, Randi, and Clarence were in the process of constructing a series of papier-mâché bromeliads that would be hung from the ceiling near the construction-paper liana vines that swooped and careened from every post and corner. Sydney and Sharon were replaying the rain forest audiotape ("Costa Rica Soundscapes," available from The Nature Conservancy, Merchandise Department, P.O. Box 294, Wye Mills, MD 21679 [1-800-382-2386]) and identifying each of the animal sounds recorded. Amanda and Carole were tracking the movements of "Hector," the class frog, who had been given residence in the makeshift aquarium on the window sill. Using a piece of graph paper, they were tracking Hector's movements to determine when he was most active and when he was least active during the course of the school day.

Moira and Lucia were dashing off to the school library to examine back issues of *Ranger Rick Magazine* to locate information on endangered wildlife that inhabited the rain forests of South America. Elaine had elected to pursue a self-initiated project that involved contacting various environmental organizations throughout the country (for example, the Rainforest Alliance [270 Lafayette St., Suite 512, New York, NY 10012], Rainforest Action Network [450 Sansome St., Suite 700, San Francisco, CA 94111], Children's Rainforest [P.O. Box 936, Lewiston, ME 04240], and The Nature Conservancy [1815 North Lynn St., Arlington, VA 22209]) to obtain information on each organization's efforts to preserve rain forest life. Emily, Tran, and Arthur were putting together a bibliography of rain forest literature that could be shared with their "pen pals" in another third grade class in Topeka.

One group of students was beginning preparations for a short video on the ecology of the rain forest. Sandra, Da'nelle, Janet, and Tim were interviewing other third grade students so they would have a list of questions to pose to the biology professor who would be visiting from the University of Kansas the following week. Abraham and Michael began looking through several books to collect information about the life of the Poison Dart Frog and other dangerous animals that lived in the rain forest canopy. Roger was constructing an "information guide" for visitors to the Brazilian rain forest.

Enthusiasm was rampant throughout the classroom. Students were excited about the opportunities to share information, discuss ideas for presenting data with other classes, and make decisions on how their "book knowledge" could be used in productive ways. Some students chose to pursue independent activities while others worked quietly in small groups. Cooperative learning was evident throughout the room as students assembled ideas and shared possibilities in an atmosphere of mutual respect and support. Competition was scarcely evident, as students helped each other with ideas, resources, and extensions of activities. It was clearly apparent that this was a true "community of learners"—one in which students were all working toward common goals, making and following through on decisions, and taking responsibility for *how* they learned as much as for *what* they learned.

Jerri's students were not engaged in haphazard activities, but rather in a well-planned and thoroughly engaging process of thematic learning. The thematic unit combined an assortment of children's literature and whole language activities into a sequential series of lessons designed to assist students in appreciating the rain forests of the world as well as the factors contributing to their destruction. Jerri had introduced the unit with a collection of books about the rain forests—including those dealing with the climate, explorations, rates of destruction, medicines obtained from rain forest plants, and some of the most unusual animals found anywhere in the world. Included in the unit were books such as *A Walk in the Rain Forest* by Kristin Pratt (Nevada City, CA: Dawn Publications, 1992); *Life in the Rain Forest* by Lucy Baker (New York: Scholastic, 1990); *Rain Forest* by Barbara Taylor (New York: Dorling Kindersley, 1992); *The Great Kapok Tree* by Lynne Cherry (San Diego: Harcourt Brace, 1990); *Tropical Rain Forests Around the World* by Elaine Landau (New York: Franklin Watts, 1991); *Welcome to the Green House* by Jane Yolen (New York: Putnam's, 1993); *Rain Forest Secrets* by Arthur Dorros (New York: Scholastic, 1990); and *Nature's Green Umbrella* by Gail Gibbons (New York: Morrow, 1994). These books (only several of the dozens selected and collected by the school librarian and other third grade teachers) were the impetus for the unit. The literature selections (for the unit) became the vehicle for a host of holistic activities. Some activities had been planned by teachers; however, a large majority were suggested by students as an outgrowth of the books read and shared in class. Some of these extending activities included:

a. the drafting of a letter to political leaders sharing students' concerns about rain forest destruction;

b. the writing of an editorial for the local newspaper;

c. a "learning vine" containing "leaves" on which were recorded new words and terms learned throughout the unit;

d. posters of selected creatures that live in each of the four major layers of the rain forest;

e. a scrapbook of amazing facts and figures;

f. a series of terrariums and aquariums containing representative rain forest flora and fauna;

g. a videotape of an interview conducted with Environmental Science majors at Kansas State University;

h. surveys of family members and relatives on environmental concerns related to rain forests;

i. an ongoing newspaper of the life and times of various rain forest inhabitants;

j. charts, graphs, and tables chronicling the rate of destruction taking place in the world's rain forest (daily, weekly, yearly); and

k. a set of informational brochures on survival tips, climatic concerns, environmental issues, and indigenous peoples.

Jerri is one of a growing legion of teachers who have discovered the enormous value and impact thematic teaching can and does have on the lives of her students. In many ways, thematic teaching allows Jerri to "energize" her curriculum and demonstrate the natural connections that exist between reading, language arts, science, social studies, math, and the creative arts. Jerri's students are also provided with opportunities to take responsibility for their learning—making choices, making decisions, and making judgments on the material and processes used throughout a designated unit. In essence, Jerri's classroom is one in which children's literature provides both a foundation and a launching pad for her students' self-initiated discoveries. A thematic unit provides breadth and depth to the entire curriculum—offering innumerable opportunities for students to become immersed in the dynamics of their own education. As we mentioned in the previous book (*The Complete Guide to Thematic Units: Creating the Integrated Curriculum*), **a thematic unit is the epitome of whole language teaching: students use language productively to answer self-initiated questions and satisfy their own inherent and natural curiosity about the world around them.**

We'd like to take a few moments to revisit some of the advantages of thematic units—for teachers (Table 1-1) as well as for students (Table 1-2).

Table 1-1

Advantages of Thematic Teaching
(for teachers)

- There is more time available for instructional purposes. Material does not have to be crammed into artificial time periods, but can be extended across the curriculum and across the day.

- The connections which can and do exist between subjects, topics, and themes can be logically and naturally developed. Teachers can demonstrate relationships and assist students in comprehending those relationships.

- Learning can be demonstrated as a continuous activity—one not restricted by textbook designs, time barriers, or even the four walls of the classroom. Teachers can help students extend learning opportunities into many aspects of their personal lives.

- Teachers are able to relinquish "control" of the curriculum and assist students in assuming a sense of "ownership" for their individual learning destinies.

- Teachers are free to help students look at a problem, situation, or topic from a variety of viewpoints, rather than the "right way" frequently demonstrated in a teacher's manual or curriculum guide.

- The development of a "community of learners" is facilitated and enhanced through thematic teaching. There is less emphasis on *competition* and more emphasis on *collaboration and cooperation*.

- Opportunities for the teacher to model appropriate learning behaviors in a supportive and encouraging environment is enhanced.

- Assessment is more holistic, authentic, and meaningful and provides a more accurate picture of students' progress and development.

- Authentic use of all the language arts (reading, writing, listening, and speaking) is encouraged throughout all curricular areas.

- There is more emphasis on *teaching* students; less emphasis on *telling* students.

- Teachers are provided with an abundance of opportunities for integrating children's literature into all aspects of the curriculum and all aspects of the day.

- Teachers can promote problem solving, creative thinking, and critical thinking processes within all aspects of a topic.

- Teachers can promote and support children's individual autonomy and self-direction by offering students control over their learning.

- Teachers are also engaged as *learners* throughout the development and implementation of a thematic unit.

Table 1-2

Advantages of Thematic Teaching
(for students)

- Focuses on the *processes* of learning moreso than the *products* of learning.

- Breaks down the "artificial barriers" that often exist between areas of the curriculum and provides an integrative approach to learning.

- Provides a child-centered curriculum—one tailored to their interests, needs, and abilities; one in which they are encouraged to make their own decisions and assume a measure of responsibility for learning.

- Stimulates self-directed discovery and investigation in and outside of the classroom.

- Assists youngsters in developing relationships between ideas and concepts, thereby enhancing appreciation and comprehension.

- Offers realistic opportunities for children to build upon individual backgrounds of information in developing new knowledge.

- Respects the individual cultural backgrounds, home experiences, and interest levels of children.

- Stimulates the creation of important concepts through first-hand experiences and self-initiated discoveries.

- Students are encouraged (and supported in their efforts) to take risks.

- Students develop more self-direction and independence through a variety of learning activities and opportunities.

- Students understand the "why" of activities and events instead of just the "what."

- Students are encouraged to make approximations of learning, rather than focus on the absolutes of learning.

- Children have sustained time and opportunity to investigate topics thoroughly and to engage in reflective inquiry.

As you can see from tables 1-1 & 1-2, thematic teaching holds enormous possibilities for both teachers and students. It opens up the elementary curriculum, facilitates the integration of subject matter, and stimulates creative and divergent thinking in a host of arenas. We sincerely believe that a well-crafted thematic unit can "energize" any classroom and provide incredible learning opportunities throughout the school day and throughout the school year.

This book is a continuation of our first book (*The Complete Guide to Thematic Units: Creating the Integrated Curriculum*). That book detailed the construction, use, and maintenance of effective thematic units, including: how to teach thematically, how to plan and organize a thematic environment, how to select appropriate themes for your students, organization tips and strategies, locating and using appropriate materials, designing "hands-on, minds-on" activities in a variety of curricular areas, and how to implement a thematic unit for maximum effectiveness. Also included were chapters on "Strategies for Success," "Authentic Assessment," and "Parent and Community Involvement." In Part II of that book, eight complete thematic units in science, social studies, language arts, and math were offered for immediate classroom use.

This volume provides additional thematic units for your use. We invite you to obtain the first volume and read the four introductory chapters to familiarize yourself with the designs and delivery systems that will help you make thematic instruction successful and meaningful for your students. The units in this book can then be used for maximum effectiveness and impact—assuring wondrous educational ventures for your students and exciting instructional opportunities for you.

We wish you great success and wonderful learning adventures as you and your students set your sails for the new horizons and endless discoveries possible through thematic instruction.

PART II:

Thematic Units

The thematic units included emphasize key concepts in either Science, Social Studies, Language Arts, or Mathematics. In addition, the activities included within each unit integrate skills from a variety of areas to ensure a unique, multidisciplinary, interdisciplinary unit of study with a strong literature component.

The chart on pages 12 and 13 lists the focus for each thematic unit, along with the various mini-themes that have been developed for each unit. These mini-themes, which can be used alone or in conjunction with other mini-units, extend the focus and concepts developed through the main thematic unit. Each mini-theme includes activities, questions, and related works of literature to provide you with a variety of choices through which to develop specific content objectives and skills.

The wide scope of activities and questions developed for each unit illustrates the tremendous possibilities from which you can select to provide students with a framework that best meets their individual needs and interests. While each unit develops a number of literary works, you may choose to use only one or two selections or you may wish to substitute other titles.

As students become involved in the various units, we suggest that you guide them in developing other activities based on classroom dynamics and teaching/learning styles. For learning to be meaningful, it must have relevance. We urge you to adapt the activities included in the units and mini-units to create a challenging and purposeful learning environment that will arouse each student's natural curiosity, and encourage all the students to pursue new ideas and formulate their own connections.

The scope of activities inherent to the thematic units and the outcomes developed will allow you to employ a wide variety of assessment techniques that not only gauge students' work but also help them grow in the process. Journals, anecdotal records, portfolio assessment, checklists, conferences, student self-evaluations, and so forth (all described in *The Complete Guide to Thematic Units: Creating the Integrated Curriculum*) provide authentic assessments that will provide an accurate assessment of students' learning and progress. We hope you will encourage your students to take an active role in both the assessment process and in determining the assessment measures for any developing unit.

Thematic Units: Themes and Mini-Themes

PRIMARY UNITS:

Topic	Focus	Mini-Themes
I. Dinosaurs (Science)	Students will explore prehistoric times to expand their knowledge of dinosaurs.	Why Dinosaurs Became Extinct The Time of the Dinosaurs Discovering Dinosaurs Other Ancient Animals
II. Special Children (Social Studies)	Students will become aware of the different types of disabilities children may have and how these children with special needs are more like other children than they are different.	Children with Physical Disabilities and/or Health Impairments Sensory Impairments Cognitively Challenged Students
III. The Caldecott Award (Language Arts)	Students will become aware of the diversity of artistic media used to illustrate children's books and become familiar with those illustrators whose books have been awarded the Caldecott Award for the most distinguished picture book published in the United States.	Maurice Sendak Ed Young Leo and Diane Dillon Chris Van Allsburg
IV. Counting and Computation (Math)	Students will develop an intuitive feeling for numbers and their various uses and interpretations.	Addition and Subtraction Large Numbers and Infinities Money Ordinal Numbers

INTERMEDIATE UNITS:

Topic	Focus	Mini-Themes
I. **Saving Our Environment** (Science)	Students will develop an awareness of the beauty of the environment as well as an understanding of the critical environmental issues that require their attention.	Saving Our Forests Endangered Species Protecting and Preserving Our Waters Trash and Garbage
II. **Multi-Cultural Understanding** (Social Studies)	Students will gain a sensitivity for the beliefs, values, and customs of other cultures.	Family Traditions Language Patterns/Dialects Struggle for Freedom Folklore
III. **Meet the Newberys** (Language Arts)	Students will become involved with Newbery Award-winning literature and the authors whose words have inspired and excited the imaginations of readers.	Introducing the Classics Award-Winning Literature Censorship and Children's Literature
IV. **Fractions** (Math)	Students will learn how fractions are an important part of our daily lives.	Decimals Cooking and Eating Money

PRIMARY UNITS

Primary Unit: Dinosaurs

Theme: DINOSAURS

Focus: Students will explore prehistoric times to expand their knowledge of dinosaurs.

Objectives: On completion of this thematic unit, students will be able to:

1.   Define various dinosaur terms such as "extinct" and "fossil."

2.   Give examples of animals from the past that are now extinct.

3.   Explain how scientists learned about life long ago.

4.   Compare/contrast life today to life when the dinosaurs existed.

Initiating Activity: Purchase 3 to 4 medium-sized watermelons and paint them white. These are then hidden in a "dinosaur nest" somewhere on the playground before the start of the lesson. Tell the students that they must find the dinosaur's nest in order to begin the dinosaur unit. Once the "eggs" are found, they can be cut open and shared with the group. After returning to the classroom, have the students draw pictures of imaginary creatures that may have laid the eggs.

General Activities:

1.   Prior to the lesson, use string to measure the height and length of various dinosaurs. Line the class up by height and choose the student in the center of the line to represent the average height. Trace this person's body on heavy butcher paper to get a pattern. On the playground, roll out the string for one of the dinosaurs. Have students guess how many bodies long and high the dinosaur is. Have a child record the estimate and use the pattern to obtain an actual measurement. Do this for the other dinosaurs for which you cut string. Compare the sizes.

2.   Have students develop different menus for various types of dinosaurs. What plants or meats must each dinosaur eat to stay healthy? How much food should a particular dinosaur eat each day?

3.   Have students work in small groups to create a large wall mural showing what life was like when the dinosaurs existed. The mural can be drawn on heavy butcher paper and decorated with paints, crayons, construction paper, or other art materials selected by the students.

4.   Make arrangements with the school "specials" teachers so that they become involved in the unit: the music teacher can teach songs related to dinosaurs; the art teacher can help students create dinosaur t-shirts using stencils and paint; the gym teacher can involve students in making

dinosaur movements; the librarian can read additional dinosaur stories and show filmstrips or movies related to dinosaurs and the age of dinosaurs.

5. Have students select a favorite dinosaur. As that dinosaur, have them write "dinograms" to another "dinosaur" in the class comparing life today with their lives during the age of dinosaurs.

6. Have students create graphs and charts that record the heights, weights, and sizes of various dinosaurs. Some library research will be necessary.

7. Invite a professor from a local college to make a short presentation on dinosaurs. Have your students prepare a list of questions beforehand to ask the visiting speaker.

8. Using known poems, songs, and stories, create frames and have the students make them into dinosaur poems and songs. For example, using *Brown Bear, Brown Bear, What Do You See?* by Bill Martin, Jr. (Holt, 1967), students can turn it into *Dinosaur, Dinosaur…* Or, students may wish to use the story, *If the Dinosaurs Came Back,* by Bernard Most (HBJ, 1978), as a model for their own story about what would happen if the dinosaurs again walked on earth.

9. Take a poll of the students' favorite dinosaurs and graph responses.

10. Share and choral read poems about dinosaurs, such as those in *Dinosaurs* (Hopkins, 1987). Have students collect their favorite dinosaur poems (both original and those published in books), illustrate them, and create a class anthology dedicated to the dinosaur.

Discussion Questions:

1. What if the dinosaurs had not become extinct?

2. What are some of the similarities between dinosaurs and some animals that live today? (Many animals have similar characteristics—for example, like the rhinoceros, triceratops walked on four legs and had horns. The hadrosaurus was a "duckbilled dinosaur" and had webbed fingers and toes. Porcupines are similar to the kentrosaurus, which was covered with sharp spikes. The pteranodon resembles the pelican—it lived by the sea and scooped up fish in a pelican-like beak. Lizards and alligators, both reptiles, have many characteristics that remind us of the dinosaurs of yesterday.)

3. How do scientists learn about animals that are no longer living? (by studying fossils and fossil tracks)

4. How can we tell if a dinosaur ate meat or plants? (Generally, the meat eaters had much sharper teeth; some even had fangs.)

5. In what ways do you think dinosaurs were able to protect themselves from their enemies? (by using their sharp teeth, claws, horns, etc.)

Literature Related Activities

Title: *The Smallest Dinosaurs*

Genre: Nonfiction

Author: Seymour Simon

Bibliographic Information: Crown, New York, 1982

Summary: Many youngsters assume that all dinosaurs were big, lumbering creatures. Not so! Many types of dinosaurs were no bigger than the pets we have at home. Simon presents valuable data on what is known and what we still have to learn about dinosaurs that weren't so big.

Interest Level: Grades 3–5.

1. Pre-Reading Activity:

   Ask students whether it would be easier for a large dinosaur or a small dinosaur to survive. Discuss the special types of survival techniques a small dinosaur would need to compete with his bigger cousins.

2. Learning Activities:

   a. Ask students to create a "testimonial" on the benefits of a small dinosaur over a large one.

   b. Have students create various small dinosaur skeletons with pipe cleaners.

   c. Have students write and illustrate make-believe stories about going back in time to observe the age of dinosaurs.

   d. Using an old board game, have students create new rules and characters for a dinosaur game.

3. Discussion Questions:

   a. What advantages did small dinosaurs have over larger ones? (They required less food; could hide more easily from enemies; could find food in certain areas inaccessible to larger dinosaurs.)

   b. What would you enjoy most about living during the time of the dinosaurs?

   c. What new information would you still like to learn about small dinosaurs?

   d. In your opinion, what is the most important thing we know about the small dinosaurs?

Title: *Digging Up Dinosaurs*

Genre: Nonfiction

Author: Aliki

Bibliographic Information: Crowell, NY, 1981

Summary: Presents readers with valuable information regarding the painstaking process of digging up dinosaur fossils and reconstructing dinosaur skeletons. The book provides data on the work of paleontologists using a light and easy tone.

Interest Level: Grades 2–4.

1. Pre-Reading Activity:

   Provide small groups of children with a pile of chicken bones (be sure the bones have been boiled and dried thoroughly). Direct each group to arrange the bones in their original configuration. Discuss any problems they had in putting the skeleton back together—even though most know exactly what a chicken looks like. Discuss the difficulties scientists have in putting a dinosaur skeleton together, particularly when no human has ever seen a live dinosaur.

2. Learning Activities:

   a. Have students imagine that they are a certain dinosaur. Have them introduce themselves to the class by describing the important features of the dinosaur they have become. Have others in the class try to determine their identities.

   b. Have students create their own dinosaur fossils. Provide small groups of students with pie plates half-filled with wet sand. Ask each group to place several chicken bones in the sand. Circular strips of cardboard can be placed around the bones and then plaster of Paris mixed and poured into the makeshift molds. After the plaster of Paris has dried, have students examine their "fossils" to note any similarities with dinosaur fossils.

   c. Have students create their own dinosaur books. Ask each student to trace an outline of a favorite type of dinosaur on a sheet of construction paper and cut it out. Students should then trace that shape on another piece of construction paper as well as several sheets of newsprint and cut them out. All the sheets should be put together (with the construction paper sheets on the front and back) and stapled together. Have students write about their favorite dinosaur on the pages of their "dinosaur book."

   d. Locate a photograph or illustration of a dinosaur skeleton. Direct students to count the number of bones in a leg, in the chest, or in other sections of the dinosaur body. Ask them to compare their count with the number of bones in a similar section of a human body or to bones in other animal groups.

3. Discussion Questions:

   a. What are some of the difficulties scientists have in reconstructing dinosaur bones? (Rarely is the entire dinosaur fossil found. Scientists have to piece together fossils like a puzzle. The skin fat and muscle of dinosaurs change into a coal-like substance and can't be examined.)

b. Why do you think people are so interested in learning about dinosaurs?

c. What do you consider to be the most interesting part of a paleontologist's job?

Title:	*Ranger Rick's Dinosaur Book*
Genre:	Nonfiction
Author:	Howard F. Robinson, Ed.
Bibliographic Information:	National Wildlife Federation, Washington, D.C., 1984
Summary:	With an abundance of illustrations and diagrams, this book provides young scientists with a captivating look at what we know about dinosaurs as well as what we postulate about dinosaurs.
Interest Level:	Grades 4–6.

---

1. Pre-Reading Activity:

   Ask each student to create an illustration of the *ideal* dinosaur. What would it look like? What size would it be in order to have the best chance for survival? What color would it be? Collect these illustrations and use them for comparison with illustrations in the book.

2. Learning Activities:

   a. Have students imagine that they are reporters who have been transported back to the time of the dinosaurs. Direct them to create a news bulletin that describes an encounter between two or more dinosaurs as they foraged in a swamp in a time long ago.

   b. Have students create an original dinosaur dictionary. Direct them to collect dinosaur-related words from this book and other resources and compile these words into a dictionary (whose papers are cut in the shape of a dinosaur).

   c. Using a long roll of butcher paper or newsprint, cover one wall of your classroom or a section of hallway outside your room. Have students create a mural that depicts the age of the dinosaurs.

3. Discussion Questions:

   a. Which dinosaur do you think would have the greatest chance for survival if it were to appear on earth today? Why? Which one would have the most difficult time surviving today? Why?

   b. Which dinosaur do you believe is the most dangerous? Why?

   c. Describe four dinosaurs to illustrate how different one dinosaur can be from another.

   d. Why do people find dinosaurs so fascinating? Which dinosaur is your favorite? Explain.

Title: *What Happened to Patrick's Dinosaur?*

Genre: Fiction

Author: Carol Carrick

Bibliographic Information: Clarion, New York, 1986

Summary: An amusing story of a boy and his dinosaur and the adventures they get into.

Interest level: Grades 1–4.

1. Pre-Reading Activity:

    Discuss with students the pros and cons of having a dinosaur for a pet.

2. Learning Activities:

    a. Discuss some of the theories used to explain the disappearance of the dinosaurs. After sharing the book with students, have them create their own books using titles such as, What Happened to _____(student's name)_____ Dinosaur?

    b. In groups have students create a skit that gives one explanation for what happened to the dinosaurs. The skit can be performed using puppets, masks, etc.

    c. Have small groups of students choose a favorite dinosaur. Ask them to take a familiar or popular song and rewrite the lyrics using dinosaur words. For example: (to the tune of "I've Been Working on the Railroad")

        > I've been watching Stegosaurus
        > All the live long day.
        > I've been watching Stegosaurus
        > Just to see what he would say.
        > Can't you hear him munchin', crunchin',
        > Rise up and start to eat a tree?
        > Don't you ever try to meet him,
        > 'Cause he will make you flee.

    d. Have students deliver a persuasive speech they would use to try to convince a parent to allow them to have a dinosaur for a pet.

3. Discussion Questions:

    a. If you were Patrick, what would you have done differently?

    b. Imagine that you went out to play one day and found a dinosaur in your back yard. What is the first thing you would say to it? What would you do?

    c. Do you think dinosaurs would make good pets? Why or why not?

    d. What if you found a clue that led you to believe a dinosaur was still living. What would you do?

Culmination: Plan a "Dinosaur Day." This day can include all or some of the following activities.

1. Have students wear dinosaur costumes or t-shirts they designed.

2. Have a dinosaur read-in—select and read only dinosaur-related books .

3. Have students write experience stories from the perspective of a dinosaur.

4. Make dinosaur models out of clay or dough mixture.

5. Play dinosaur games and sing dinosaur songs.

6. Show a dinosaur movie such as *The Land Before Time.*

7. Have a dinosaur feast making dinosaur-shaped foods out of jello, cookie dough, etc.

8. Construct and break open a dinosaur piñata.

9. Invite a guest speaker from a museum or local college to speak about dinosaurs.

10. Go on a field trip to a fossil site or local museum.

11. Create a "Dinosaur Book of World Records" (largest, smallest, heaviest, smallest brain, most ferocious, etc.).

12. Create dinosaur coloring books to share with other students.

13. Put together a traveling dinosaur museum filled with artifacts, books, pictures, etc. collected and created during this unit. Display it during the "Dinosaur Day" festivities and then have the museum go on tour throughout the school.

Supplemental Literature

Primary (Grades 1–3):

Aliki. (1985). *Dinosaurs are different.* New York: Crowell, 1985.

> The major differences between dinosaurs are discussed through an examination of their bones and skeletons. A "must" for any dinosaur hunter.

Barton, B. (1990). *Bones, bones, dinosaur bones.* New York: HarperCollins.

> An ideal book for very young readers. It offers a glimpse into the search for dinosaur bones as well as how dinosaur skeletons are constructed.

Barton, B. (1989). *Dinosaurs, dinosaurs.* New York: Crowell.

> All kinds of dinosaurs—from big to small, horned to armored, long necked and long tailed—are detailed in this wonderful introduction to the world of dinosaurs.

Carroll, S. (1986). *How big is a Brachiosaurus?* New York: Platt and Munk.

> Using a question-and-answer format, the author presents important information on the physical characteristics, eating habits, and living conditions of various dinosaurs.

Craig, J. (1989). *Discovering prehistoric animals.* Mahwah, NJ: Troll.

> A simple, straightforward text filled with lots of down-to-earth facts about dinosaurs.

Hopkins, L. B. (1987). *Dinosaurs*. San Diego, CA: Harcourt Brace.

Eighteen poems give students some fresh perspectives and delightful insights into the world of dinosaurs.

Lauber, P. (1987). *Dinosaurs walked here: And other stories fossils tell*. New York: Bradbury.

Everything the young scientist would want to know about fossils can be found in this enlightening book.

Most, B. (1978). *If the dinosaurs came back*. San Diego: H.B.J.

An imaginative look at life today if the dinosaurs returned.

Peters, D. (1989). *A gallery of dinosaurs and other early reptiles*. New York: Knopf.

The emphasis in this book is on size, with a wonderful collection of colorful illustrations and gatefold pages to describe the enormity of these giants.

Prelutsky, J. (1988). *Tyrannosaurus was a beast*. Illustrated by A. Lobel. New York: Mulberry Brown.

Poems about dinosaurs—from Ankylosaurus to Seismosuras, and more!

Robinson, H. (1984). *Ranger Rick's dinosaur book*. Washington, D.C.: National Wildlife Federation.

Filled with lots of colorful illustrations and photos, this book offers young scientists a wealth of data about all kinds of dinosaurs.

Intermediate (Grades 4–6):

Arnold, C. (1990). *Dinosaurs down under: And other fossils from Australia*. New York: Clarion.

This book describes some of the dinosaurs that were found in Australia.

Branley, F. (1982). *Dinosaurs, asteroids, and superstars: Why the dinosaurs disappeared*. New York: Crowell.

The continuing mystery surrounding the disappearance of the dinosaurs is examined in this informative book.

Cobb, V. (1983). *The monsters who died: A mystery about dinosaurs*. New York: Coward-McCann.

A perceptive and engaging look into reasons why the dinosaurs died, this book also explains how fossils have helped us understand these creatures.

Cohen, D. (1983). *Monster dinosaur*. New York: Lippincott.

This books emphasizes the work of paleontologists and describes both understandings and misconceptions that have developed over the years regarding dinosaurs.

Freedman, R. (1983). *Dinosaurs and their young*. New York: Holiday.

This book focuses on dinosaur families and dispels some of the myths about dinosaurs as solitary creatures.

Gurney, J. (1992). *Dinotopia*. New York: Turner.

The exciting adventures of Professor Denison and his son, Will, in Dinotopia, a land where dinosaurs and humans live in peaceful coexistence.

Jacobs, F. (1982). *Supersaurus*. New York: Putnam.

The discoveries one paleontologist makes in Colorado lead to the discovery of the remains of one of the largest dinosaurs that ever lived.

Lasky, K. (1990). *Dinosaur dig*. New York: Morrow.

> Several families are involved in the search for dinosaur fossils in this description of a "dig" in the Montana Badlands.

Sattler, H. (1989). *Tyrannosaurus Rex and its kin: The Mesozoic monsters*. New York: Lothrop.

> This book examines the most famous of all dinosaurs and takes a look at all the related descendants of Tyrannosaurus Rex. Colorful illustrations and a time chart are highlights.

Sattler, H. (1990). *The new illustrated dinosaur dictionary*. New York: Lothrop.

> It's all here! Everything any dinosaur "nut" would want to know about over 350 dinosaurs and other related creatures.

MINI-THEMES

Why Dinosaurs Became Extinct

There are many different reasons offered to explain the extinction of the dinosaurs. Some of the more popular ones include: a sudden change in the Earth's climate; a loss of food; and the collision of an enormous meteor with the Earth. Although scientists disagree as to *the* reason for the disappearance of dinosaurs, students will enjoy reading about these theories and offering their own explanations for this phenomena.

References

Barton, B. (1989). *What happened to the dinosaurs*. New York: Crowell.

Branley, F. (1982). *Dinosaurs, asteroids, and superstars: Why the dinosaurs disappeared*. New York: Crowell.

Branley, F. (1989). *What happened to the dinosaurs?* New York: Crowell.

Cobb, V. (1983). *The monsters who died: A mystery about dinosaurs*. New York: Coward-McCann.

Elting, M. and Goodman, A. (1980). *Dinosaur mysteries*. New York: Platt and Munk.

Simon, S. (1990). *New questions and answers about dinosaurs*. New York: Morrow.

Activities

1. Have students correspond with another class in another state (addresses can be obtained from current issues of *Learning Magazine* and *Teaching K-8 Magazine*). Ask students to explain why they believe the dinosaurs became extinct and have them ask their pen pals to respond to this theory.

2. Have each student select a dinosaur and, as this creature, write a letter explaining why he/she would or would not like to live in today's world.

3. Contact the debate team or club at your local high school or college to determine if its students would be willing to debate the theories related to the disappearance of the dinosaurs. Make a videotape of the debate to share with other classes.

4. Invite a local paleontologist from a nearby college to visit your classroom and share his /her theory to explain the disappearance of the dinosaurs. Have students prepare questions they would like the guest speaker to address.

The Time of the Dinosaurs

During the time of the dinosaurs, the earth looked much different than it does today. Land bridges between continents, massive inland seas, and strange plant life dominated the landscape. Students will enjoy looking at the world as it was during the time of the dinosaurs.

References

Arnold, C. (1990). *Dinosaur mountain: Graveyard of the past.* New York: Clarion.

Carroll, S. (1986). *How big is a Brachiosaurus?* New York: Platt and Munk.

Milton, J. (1985). *Dinosaur days.* New York: Random House.

Sattler, H. (1981). *Dinosaurs of North America.* New York: Lothrop.

Sattler, H. (1989). *Tyrannosaurus Rex and its kin: The Mesozoic monsters.* New York: Lothrop.

Activities

1. Provide students with empty shoe boxes, various pieces of colored construction paper, glue, scissors, and other art materials. Ask students (individually or in small groups) to design dioramas of selected prehistoric scenes.

2. Have each student take on the role of a selected dinosaur. Invite each student to record a day in the life of this dinosaur. What do they eat? What do they do all day? What surprises do they encounter?

3. Read *Dinosaurs and their Young* by Russell Freedman (New York: Holiday, 1983), to the entire class. This book discusses the family life of hadrosaurs and describes some of their enemies. After the reading, involve students in a discussion that focuses on comparisons between the family life of dinosaurs and that of other wild and/or domesticated animals.

4. Obtain a copy of the sound filmstrip series," Plants and Animals of Long Ago" (Catalog No. C30165, National Geographic Society, Washington, DC 20036; telephone: 1-800-368-2728). Have students discuss some of the most interesting, and what they consider important, information presented in the filmstrip.

Discovering Dinosaurs

New discoveries about dinosaurs are being made every day. Paleontologists and other scientists are digging up dinosaurs and other ancient creatures around the world—many of these discoveries are making the front page of our local newspapers. The careers involved in dinosaur discoveries and how these scientists work are covered in this mini-theme.

References

Aliki. (1981). *Digging up dinosaurs*. New York: Crowell.

Aliki. (1988). *Dinosaur bones*. New York: Crowell.

Aliki. (1990). *Fossils tell of long ago*. New York: HarperCollins.

Barton, B. (1989). *Bones, bones, dinosaur bones*. New York: HarperCollins.

Cohen, D. (1983). *Monster dinosaur*. New York: Lippincott.

Gilbert, J. (1981). *Dinosaurs discovered*. New York: Larousse.

Lasky, K. (1990). *Dinosaur dig*. New York: Morrow:

Lauber, P. (1987). *Dinosaurs walked here: And other stories fossils tell*. New York: Bradbury.

Activities

1. Contact your district's high school and ask to borrow any fossils they may have for display. Show these to students and help them create their own fossils. Provide each student with modeling clay and a variety of leaves. Have students flatten out their clay and place a selected leaf into the clay. Have them carefully remove the leaves from the clay and discuss the impressions made in the clay. Discuss how these are similar to or different from the impressions made by living things of ancient times.

2. Have students create several big books. The front and back covers of each can be cut from stiff cardboard into the shape of a selected dinosaur. Sheets of paper can also be cut into the same pattern as the cover and stapled between the cardboard. Each book can be a record of important data about the selected dinosaur. The completed books can eventually be donated to the school library, or be part of a visiting book collection that goes to various classrooms.

3. Have students brainstorm all the adjectives they can think of to describe dinosaurs and list these on the board. Next, have students offer an antonym for each adjective listed. Have them select several adjectives and their antonyms and create an "Attribute Chart" (see below). Have student select several dinosaurs and "rate" each according to how it "measures up" on the chart.

Tyrannosaurus Rex

Huge ..X .... Small

Meat-eater ..X .... Plant-eater

Sharp Teeth.X .... No Teeth

Ferocious .... X .... Gentle

4. Obtain a copy of the video, "Dinosaurs: Puzzles from the Past" (Catalog No. C51046, National Geographic Society, Washington, DC 20036; telephone: 1-800-368-2728). Discuss with students how information in the film is similar to or different from that discovered in the selected books.

Other Ancient Animals

Dinosaurs certainly weren't the only animals that lived long ago. Mammoths, Mastodons, Pterodactyls and other strange creatures were also part of the history of the earth. Although most appeared after the dinosaurs died out, they are still a source of fascination for many students.

References

Craig, J. (1989). *Discovering prehistoric animals.* Mahwah, NJ: Troll.

Knight, D.C. (1985). *"Dinosaurs" that swam and flew.* New York: Prentice.

Sattler, H. (1985). *Pterosaurs, the flying reptiles.* New York: Lothrop.

Selsam, M. (1977). *Sea monsters of long ago.* New York: Four Winds.

Zallinger, P. (1978). *Prehistoric animals.* New York: Random House.

Activities

1. Have students survey teachers, administrators, and other adults about all dinosaurs and other ancient creatures with which they are familiar. What ancient animals are cited most often? The collected data can be arranged in the form of a bar or line graph.

2. Using paper bags and various colors of construction paper, allow each student to construct a prehistoric animal puppet. When the puppets are completed, separate the students into groups of four. In small groups, students can write and design a play using their puppets as the main characters.

3. Many prehistoric animals have features similar to animals of today (for example, the mammoth shares characteristics with the elephant). Have students construct a large bulletin board display. On one half of the bulletin board, pictures and illustrations of ancient animals can be posted. The other half of the bulletin board can display illustrations and photos of today's animals. Yarn can be used to link the prehistoric animals with existing animals they most resemble.

4. Have students create Venn diagrams to compare a prehistoric animal with its more current "cousin."

Primary Unit: Special Children

Theme: SPECIAL CHILDREN

Focus: Students will become aware of the different types of disabilities children may have and how these children with special needs are more like other children than different.

Objectives: On completion of this thematic unit, students will be able to:

1. Become familiar with different types of disabilities.

2. Increase their awareness and acceptance of all children as individuals with disabilities.

3. Recognize that all people have similarities and differences as well as strengths and weaknesses.

4. Accept differences in others as well as in themselves.

Initiating Activity: Discuss how important it is to know that each person is special. Tell the students ways in which you think you are special. Ask them to tell you ways in which they think they are special. Pair students and ask them to identify something special about their partner. Then ask each child to introduce his or her partner by saying, *"This is John. He is special because he..."*

General Activities:

1. Provide the children with large sheets of paper. Ask them to pretend that they are one of the characters, with a disability, from the books they've been reading, for example, Philip, the new kid from *Arnie and the New Kid* or someone they know with a disability. Once they have identified the character or person and his or her disability, write the character's or person's name on the paper and then tell the children to illustrate things they currently enjoy doing that they *could not* do if they had the disability of the character/person identified. When they have completed their illustrations, allow them to work in pairs or small groups so they can discuss possible ways they could do the things they illustrated and/or to think of alternative activities they could do.

2. Ask the children to think about their best friend and the friendship they share. Then discuss, with the children, whether they think the friendship would change if suddenly the friend developed some type of disability. If so, what would be different? Why? Then turn it around and ask the children to imagine themselves with a disability and ask them if they feel the friendship would change in anyway. Allow time for them to write a brief story about one of these two situations— a friend being disabled or them being disabled. Share the stories.

3. Ask the children to think about changes and accommodations that would need to be made in their homes if someone who lived there was in a wheelchair. Provide the children with a large sheet of paper and ask them to make a drawing of their home with the accommodations.

4. Assign children to work in pairs with someone they know well for the following activity. Each of the children should fold a piece of paper in half lengthwise. On one side of the paper ask the children to write or illustrate ways in which they are alike or the same as their partner. On the other half of the paper, write or illustrate how they are different. This should be done independent of each other. Then allow time for them to share their papers with each other and

see how much they agree or disagree. Finally, as a group discuss how *all* people (people with or without disabilities) are different, in some way and yet very much alike in other ways.

5. Discuss with the children that *all* people are special in one way or another. Tell the children to write the letters of their name down the side of a sheet of paper. Next, ask them to think of a word that starts with each letter of their name that they could use in a phrase or sentence to describe how special they are.

    EXAMPLE: L—Lovely   I am special because I do lovely things for people.

    I—Ice Cream   I am special because I share my ice cream with my brother.

    Z—Zebra   I am special because I have a pet zebra and everyone likes to pet him.

    Next ask the children to do this same activity, using the letters of a friend's name.

6. To further reinforce the idea that everyone has something that is special about them, ask the children to draw a picture of their family, group of friends, or neighbors. Then ask them to write (for each person they included in their picture) in sentence form, the following: "_____ (name of person) is special because _____." Allow time to share.

7. Many of the stories in this unit are about people who are different in some way. Create a bulletin board by placing the words "SAME" and "DIFFERENT" on separate halves of the bulletin board. Ask students to identify ways in which they are the same as others and ways in which they are different, for example, *some people have long hair, some short; some have blue eyes, others brown.* Emphasize that it is okay to be different. Then tell the students to cut pictures of all types of people from magazines and attach them to the bulletin board to illustrate how alike and yet different all people are.

8. Almost everyone has something about them or their bodies that they don't particularly like, for example, *ugly feet, a crooked tooth, a birth mark, etc.* Discuss how people often try to keep their "imperfection" a secret by not allowing whatever it is to show. Talk about how disabled people probably don't like some of the things that are wrong with them, but they can't always keep it a secret. Write the following letter on the chalkboard:

    Dear Children,

    Hello, my name is Carlos. I have a crooked tooth. I used to not smile because I didn't want anyone to see it. Now I smile anyway because people like me even with a crooked tooth. I hope you will write to me and tell me about yourself. Goodbye, Carlos.

    Ask the children to write a letter to Carlos and then to share (only if they want to) with the group.

Discussion Questions:

1. Have you ever felt different from other people? If so, when and why? Explain. (Answers may vary.)

2. In what ways are people all alike? Explain. (Answers may vary.)

3. How do you feel when you see someone who has a disability or someone who looks and acts differently than you do? Explain. (Answers may vary.)

4. How would your life change if you were in an accident and became physically disabled (for example, you couldn't walk, lost a limb, or the like)? (Answers may vary.)

5. How do people become disabled? (Answers may vary, but might include because of an accident or because they were born that way.)

Literature Related Activities

Title:	*Arnie and the New Kid*
Genre:	Picture Book
Author:	Nancy Carlson
Bibliographic Information:	Penguin Books USA Inc., New York, 1990
Summary:	Philip, a new kid (cat) at school is different from most kids (cats) at school and doesn't have many friends. He is in a wheelchair and "top cat" Arnie teases him about it. Then Arnie falls down the school steps and breaks a leg, twists a wrist, and sprains his tail. He then begins to see life from a different perspective.
Interest Level:	Grades K–2.

1. Pre-Reading Activity:

    Show the children the cover of the book and ask them to describe what they see. Ask them to tell you about someone they know or have seen in a wheelchair. Read the title, *Arnie and the New Kid*, and ask them to predict what they think will happen between Arnie and the "New Kid."

2. Learning Activities:

    a. There were some things Arnie and Philip could do together and other things they could not do together. Ask the children to fold a piece of paper in half, then on one side write "*Things I could do with someone in a wheelchair,*" and on the other half write "*Things I could not do with someone in a wheelchair.*" Then tell the children to write or illustrate the activities they could or could not do on the appropriate sides of the paper. As a group, share and discuss all the activities that could be done with someone in a wheelchair, noting that there are many.

    b. Write the dedication of the book, "*For Barry… who, just like Arnie, teased someone and learned his lesson*" on the chalkboard and then choral read it. Discuss what they think this dedication means. Then ask them whether they think it is a good dedication for this story and why or why not. Finally, as a group, create another dedication for this book.

    c. Point out to the children that they often tease and make fun of each other. In this story, Arnie made fun of Philip because he was in a wheelchair. Ask the children to write about how they feel when someone teases them *or* when they tease someone else. Allow time to share these incidents and feelings.

   d. Let the students role play a situation in which one of them is in a wheelchair, another one
       is not, and a third student is teasing the one in the wheelchair. What would they do and say?
       Allow them to act out the situation, giving several students an opportunity to play each role.

3. Discussion Questions:

   a. It was said in the book that Philip was different from most kids. What was different about
       him? (Answers may vary, but might include because he was in a wheelchair and needed help
       doing some things.)

   b. Why did Arnie tease Philip? (Answers may vary, but might include because he was in a
       wheelchair and couldn't do some of the things other kids could do.) How do you feel about
       the way Arnie teased Philip? (Answers may vary.)

   c. Do you think Arnie will continue to tease other kids who are different? Why or why not?
       (Answers may vary.)

   d. Who would you rather have as a friend, Arnie or Philip? Explain. (Answers may vary.)

Title: *Mandy*

Genre: Realistic Fiction

Author: Barbara Booth

Illustrator: Jim Lamarche

Bibliographic Information: Lothrop, Lee, and Shepard Books, New York, 1991

Summary: Mandy, a hearing impaired girl, and her grandmother enjoy doing many things
                        together. Grandmother loses her beloved pin and Mandy risks going out on a scary,
                        stormy night to look for it.

Interest Level: Grades 1–4.

---

1. Pre-Reading Activity:

   Mandy's grandmother had a pin that was very special to her. When she lost it, she felt sad. Ask
   the children to think about a time when they lost something that was special to them. What did
   they do? Did anybody help them look for it? Did they find it? Ask the children to predict whether
   or not Grandma's pin will be found. If it is found, who will find it?

2. Learning Activities:

   a. Ask the children to fold a sheet of paper in half. On one half, tell them to draw something
       Mandy liked to do with her grandmother. On the other side, tell the children to identify
       someone they like doing something with and to illustrate or write about what it is. Next, help
       the children write letters to the people they identified telling them about the things they like
       to do with them.

b. Grandma loved her pin because it was something Grandpa had given her on their 25th wedding anniversary. Ask the children to think of something they have that is special to them because it brings back special memories. Discuss that their *"special thing"* might be something that has been passed down in the family. Send a letter home to the parents explaining what you are doing, then set aside a day for sharing these *"special things."* Finally, ask the children to pretend that they lost their *"special thing"* on the way home from school, and to write a brief story about what they'd do and illustrate it. Allow time to share these stories.

c. Mandy is a nickname for Amanda. Mandy loved her nickname because when people said her name *"their lips curled up at the ends almost like a smile."* Discuss how nicknames are often part of the real name, but can also be a name that may describe something about a person or simply be a name someone decided to call another person for a variety of reasons. Ask the children, if they want, to share their nicknames, and how they got them, with the group.

d. Mandy had a favorite picture that had *"Grandpa and Amanda—age 2½"* written under it. Ask the children to bring in a favorite picture of themselves that was taken with at least one other person. Allow time for the children to share.

3. Discussion Questions:

a. Mandy had never heard anyone talk or sing. What do you think it would be like not to be able to hear or talk? (Answers may vary.)

b. How did Mandy and her Grandma "talk" with each other? (Answers may vary, but might include through sign language, lip reading, pointing, and expressions.)

c. Why did Mandy go back to look for Grandma's pin? (Answers may vary.) Do you think it was a good idea for her to do that? Why, or why not?

d. Why did Mandy hate the dark? (Answers may vary, but might include because she couldn't hear sounds so people and/or animals startled her.)

Title: *Michael*

Genre: Fantasy

Author: Tony Bradman

Bibliographic Information: Macmillan, New York, 1990

Summary: Michael is different from all of the other students. He is late and is frequently in trouble. Michael, however, makes something that surprises everyone.

Interest Level: Grades K–3.

1. Pre-Reading Activity:

Michael's behavior was different from that of other students. As a group, brainstorm about behaviors that are different but acceptable and behaviors that are different but unacceptable. Write these behaviors on the chalkboard in two different columns. Then discuss why some behaviors are acceptable and others are not. Also, point out that some behaviors may be acceptable in one situation or setting but not in another or that some behaviors are acceptable to some people but not to others.

2. Learning Activities:

    a. Ask the children to identify what Michael invented in the story and to think about what he will invent next. Then ask them to think of something they would like to invent. Encourage the students to think of things that are real and not real. Next, tell them to fold a piece of paper in half. On one side, ask them to draw a picture of something they would like to invent and then to name it. On the other side draw something they think Michael will invent and name it. Display the illustrations.

    b. Ask the students to work in small groups and develop a travel brochure of where they think Michael will land his rocket ship. The travel brochure should include the name of the city and state where he will land and a paragraph describing the key information about that city and state. Also, a picture of where he will land can be drawn or cut out of a magazine.

    c. Remind the children about the letter Michael wrote while he was traveling in his rocket ship. Write the following letter on the chalkboard and choral read it:

        Dear Students,

        I like my rocket ship a lot because I can travel real fast. The only thing I don't like is that it is too small and I am running out of room. I hope I come down to earth real soon. Also, I forgot to put very much food in the rocket ship before I left and now I am a little hungry. But I do like being in here because I can see out my window and it is very beautiful. I hope all is well. Please write to me. Sincerely.

        Then as a group, write an answer to Michael's letter.

    d. In Michael's letter, he said he was hungry. Ask the students to pretend that when Michael returns to school they will have a party for him. Then plan the party by doing the following:

        •   Make a list of who should be invited to the party.

        •   Make a list of what food should be served.

        •   What should they write on the top of a cake for Michael?

        •   As a group, write a short speech to welcome Michael back.

        You may assign different tasks to different groups or plan the party as a whole group. You may want to role play Michael's homecoming and actually have a party!

3. Discussion Questions:

    a. What did you like most about Michael? What did you like least about him? (Answers may vary.)

    b. Would you like to have Michael for a friend? Why or why not? (Answers may vary.)

    c. Michael's teachers said he was *"the worst boy in the school."* What kinds of things did Michael do that made him *"the worst boy in the school"*? (He was late for school; he was scruffy; he didn't listen to the teachers or do what they said; he liked to read but not what the teachers asked him to read.) Do you agree with what the teachers said about him? Why or why not? (Answers may vary.)

    d. What are some of the things that happened in this story that would most likely happen and which things would most likely not happen? (Answers may vary.)

Title:	*Our Brother Has Down's Syndrome*
Genre:	Informational
Authors:	Shelley Cairo, Jasmine Cairo, and Tara Cairo
Photographer:	Irene McNirl
Bibliographic Information:	Annick Press Ltd., Toronto, Canada, 1991
Summary:	Tara and Jasmine have a little brother named Jai. He has Down's Syndrome. They tell their story about how he is very much like every other brother or sister in the world.
Interest Level:	Grades 1–3.

1. Pre-Reading Activities:

In this story, Tara and Jasmine tell about their younger brother, Jai. Have the students talk about their brothers and/or sisters. Ask them what they like best about having a brother/sister and what they like least. After reading the story, talk about how similar and how different their feelings are compared with those of Tara and Jasmine.

2. Learning Activities:

    a. Invite a nurse/doctor to come to the classroom to discuss Down's Syndrome. Have them talk about how a child is born with Down's Syndrome and what we *can and cannot* do for children with Down's Syndrome.

    b. As a group, create a thank you note to send to Jasmine and Tara Cairo via the publisher (Annick Press Ltd., Toronto, Canada M2M 1H9) thanking them for sharing the story about their special brother. In the thank you note, the children may want to tell them about someone they know who is special in their own family, at school, a neighbor, etc.

    c. Jai's sister wrote this story about him. Discuss with the children how they think Jai felt about his sisters. Then, as a group, ask the children to pretend that they are Jai and to write a story about his sisters Jasmine and Tara.

    d. Tell the students that Jai has Down's Syndrome. Ask the students if they can get *"Down's Syndrome"* from Jai by touching or playing with him. With the students, make a list of things you can *"catch"* from other children and things you cannot.

3. Discussion Questions:

    a. What was special about Jai? (He has Down's Syndrome.) What does it mean to have Down's Syndrome? (The person has 47 chromosomes in each cell.) Do you know anyone who has Down's Syndrome? (Answers may vary.)

    b. Is there a way to make Down's Syndrome go away? (No.) What can you do to help people with Down's Syndrome? (Answers may vary, but might include help them by playing with them and talking to them and giving them lots of love.)

    c. Tara and Jasmine say that other kids and grown-ups sometimes make fun of Jai. Why do you think they do that? What could you say to them that might get them to stop? (Answers may vary.)

    d. Why do you think Jasmine and Tara wanted to tell this story about their brother? (Answers may vary.)

Culmination: The culminating activity will be a discussion/display of what makes this class of children special. Ask the children to think about some of the things that make them special and then complete the following statements.

I am special because I wear _____

I am special because I can _____

I am special because I like _____

I am special because I have _____

I am special because my friend _____

I am special because I do _____

Other things that make me special are _____

Draw a picture of yourself being a special person.

Display worksheets and discuss.

Supplemental Literature

Primary (Grades 1–3):

Brown, T. (1984). *Someone special, just like you.* New York: Henry Holt.

> This book contains wonderful photographs of children doing the things children like to do best, but the children in the photographs have handicaps. The story demonstrates that although they may not walk, talk, hear, or see the way others do, that doesn't make them different in their need to experience life completely.

Bunnett, R. (1993). *Friends in the park.* New York: Checkerboard Press.

> A warm and sensitive text that invites the reader to join a group of young children with all kinds of abilities during a day at the park.

Chapman, E. (1982). *Suzy.* Illustrated by Margery Gill. London, England: The Bodley Head.

> Suzy is partially sighted. She finds it difficult to see things clearly, especially when they are at a distance. She reads large-type books and needs to use a magnifying glass to see words and letters. She prefers swimming to playing ball because she has difficulty seeing the ball.

Dwight, L. (1992). *We can do it.* New York: Checkerboard.

> A book about five special children and what they can do. It is an inspiring book with engaging photographs.

Kraus, R. (1971). *Leo the late bloomer.* Photographs by Jose Aruego. New York: Simon & Schuster.

> Leo was a little tiger cub who could not do things other young animals could do, such as read, write, draw, and speak. Leo's parents recognized that he was a late bloomer, however. His father worries about him and keeps anxiously watching him all year long. Finally, one day Leo "blooms" and everyone is happy.

Lasker, J. (1974). *He's my brother.* Morton Grove, IL: Albert Whitman & Co.

> Jamie has a learning disability. In this story, his older brother describes how things are for him at home and at school.

Levine, E.S. (1974). *Lisa and her soundless world.* New York: Human Science Press.

> This is a story about how an eight-year-old's deafness is diagnosed and how it affects her life. This unique book fulfills a need for creating understanding attitudes toward deafness.

London, J. (1992). *The lion who had asthma.* Illustrated by Nadine Bernard Westcott. Morton Grove, IL: Albert Whitman & Co.

> This book includes information on childhood asthma and how to control its symptoms. As Sean, the boy with asthma, flies his imaginary plane, he wears a nebulizer mask that aids in his recovery following an asthma attack.

Merrifield, M. (1990). *Come sit by me.* Illustrated by Heather Collins. Toronto, Canada: Women's Press.

> This is a beautifully illustrated, sensitive, and realistic book about a young girl who finds out one of her schoolmates has AIDS.

Raskin, E. (1968). *Spectacles.* New York: Atheneum Publishers.

> Iris sees some strange things—such as a fire-breathing dragon, a giant pygmy nuthatch, and a fat kangaroo—because she can't see things clearly. Iris's mother takes her to an eye doctor for an eye

exam. After some resistance to wearing glasses, Iris realizes that she can see better with glasses on and enjoys it.

Russo, M. (1992). *Alex is my friend*. New York: Greenwillow Books.

This is the story of two young boys who are friends. One of the boys, Alex, is much smaller than the other even though he is older. Alex has an operation and is less able to run and walk and sometimes needs to use a wheelchair. The boys remain friends and their interests change as Alex become less physically able.

Schwartz, C. (1992). *Shelley the hyperactive turtle*. Rockville, MD: Woodbine House.

Shelley, a little turtle, has a difficult time staying still and always feels jumpy and wiggly inside. Shelley's mother takes him to a doctor, who explains that Shelley is hyperactive. Shelley begins to understand why he is different from other turtles and, with treatment, begins to improve.

Stein, S.B. (1974). *About handicaps: An open family book for parents and children together*. New York: Walker & Co.

This is an excellent first book to introduce the topic of individuals who are exceptional. This book focuses on individuals with physical disabilities, but many of the ideas and considerations expressed in this book reflect a broader group of exceptionalities. This sensitive book portrays a realistic representation of how young children feel when they encounter persons with physical disabilities.

Wright, B.R. (1981). *My sister is different*. Illustrated by Helen Cogancherry. Shaker Heights, OH: Raintree Publisher.

A young brother, Carlo, struggles with his positive and negative feelings about his mentally handicapped sister, Terry. It is not until he almost loses her that he realizes how special Terry really is.

Intermediate (Grades 4–6):

Alexander, S.H. (1990). *Mom can't see me*. Photos by George Ancona. New York: Macmillan.

A nine-year-old girl describes how her mother leads a productive and rich life despite being blind.

Avi (1992). *Man from the sky*. New York: Morrow Jr. Books.

This is a suspenseful story about three distinctly different people.

Betancourt, J. (1993). *My name is Brian*. New York: Scholastic.

Brian struggles with his difficulty with reading and his new sixth-grade teacher who labels him as learning disabled.

Birdseye, T. (1993). *Just call me stupid*. New York: Holiday House.

Like many children who have difficulty with reading, Patrick avoids any situation in which he might be expected to read or interact with books. However, a friendship with a neighbor girl who reads aloud to him helps him to become excited about books.

Cassedy, S. (1987). *M.E. and Morton*. New York: Thomas Y. Crowell.

An eleven-year-old girl is ashamed that her older brother is a slow learner. However, although she wanted a friend of her own, a very flamboyant new girl picks the brother instead of her as a friend.

Gallico, P. (1992). *The snow goose*. Minnesota: Knopf.

This is a tale about the friendship between a hunchbacked artist, a child, and an injured snow goose that needs to be nursed. The book is beautifully illustrated with impressionistic paintings.

Greenfield, E. and Revis, A. (1981). *Alesia*. New York: Philomel.

This is a true story about a physically disabled young girl who discusses the accident that left her crippled and her feelings about her disability.

Kesey, K. *The sea lion*. Illustrated by Neil Waldman. New York: Viking Penguin.

Although Eemook suffered because of his small size and bad leg, he proved his worth by saving his tribe from an evil and powerful spirit that came visiting one stormy night.

Krementz, J. (1992). *How it feels to live with a physical disability*. New York: Simon & Schuster.

A powerful and heartwarming story about the indomitable spirit of children who live with physical disabilities.

Pollock, P. (1982). *Keeping it secret*. New York: G.P. Putnam's Sons.

Because of her attempt to hide her hearing aid, Mary Lou adjusts poorly to her new school and refuses several overtures of friendship. With help from her family, she finally decides that the only barrier to making new friends is her own attitude.

Roy, R. (1985). *Move over, wheelchair coming through!* New York: Clarion Books.

This book presents seven disabled youths between the ages of nine and nineteen who use wheelchairs. These youths all lead fully active lives at home, at school, and on vacation.

Walker, L.A. (1994). *Hand, heart, and mind: The story of the education of America's deaf people*. New York: Dial.

This book traces the history of America's deaf people from its roots in ancient times to the effects of the 1988 student revolt at Gallaudet University.

Wood, J.R. (1992). *The man who loved clowns*. New York: G.P. Putnam's Sons.

A thirteen-year-old girl makes herself invisible around people because she is embarrassed about her handicapped uncle who lives with her family.

MINI-THEMES

Children with Physical Disabilities and/or Health Impairments

There are two major reasons why children are physically disabled or have health impairments—either they were born that way or had an accident. Children with physical disabilities have difficulties with the structure or functioning of their body. Children with health impairments have ongoing medical problems that require regular medical attention. Examples of physical and health impairments include: *asthma, cerebral palsy, HIV infection, spina bifida, muscular dystrophy, multiple sclerosis, and cystic fibrosis.* Most children with physical and health difficulties have average or above intelligence and are extremely capable of learning and succeeding in a regular classroom. They can also lead fairly normal lives. By reading the following books and completing the suggested activities, children can learn about different types of physical disabilities and health impairments and how the children inflicted with them live relatively normal lives.

References

Aiello, B. (1988). *Friends for life.* Frederick, MD: Twenty-first Century Books.

Aiello, B. (1988). *It's your turn at bat.* Frederick, MD: Twenty-first Century Books.

Alexander, S.H. (1992). *Mom's best friend.* New York: Macmillan.

Bergman, T. (1989). *On our own terms.* Milwaukee, WI: Gareth Stevens Children's Books.

Caseley, J. (1991). *Harry and Willy Carrothead.* New York: Greenwillow Books.

Dugan, B. (1992). *Loop the loop.* New York: Greenwillow Books.

Durant, P.R. (1992). *When heroes die.* New York: Viking.

Emmert, M. (1992). *I'm the big sister now.* Chicago, IL: Whitman.

Fassler, J. (1975). *Howie helps himself.* Chicago, IL: Whitman.

Fassler, D. and McQueen, K. (1990). *What's a virus, anyway? A kids' book about AIDS.* Burlington, VT: Waterfront Books.

Girard, L.W. (1992). *Alex, the kid with AIDS.* Chicago, IL: Whitman.

Rodgers, A. (1987). *Luke has asthma, too.* Burlington, VT: Waterfront Books.

Wolf, B. (1974). *Don't feel sorry for Paul.* New York: J.B. Lippincott Co.

Activities

1. Discuss with the children that it is a law that public buildings must have ramps or elevators for people in wheelchairs so they can get to where they want to go. Ask the children if they think this is important or not. Next, ask the children what other things can be done to make it easier for people in wheelchairs (for example, lower drinking fountains).

    Ask the children, for the next week, as they go to the grocery, doctor, dentist, shopping, etc., to look for accommodations that have been made to buildings to enable access for people with disabilities, for example, ramps, lowered drinking fountains, handrails. Tell them to illustrate or make a list of the places and types of accommodations and to bring the illustration or list to school by a designated date. Once the children bring their illustrations or lists to school, discuss what they saw and compile the data. As a group, you may want to write a letter to the appropriate person in your community telling him/her about your concern about lack of access to buildings or to compliment him/her if the access is good.

2. Each year there are marathon races for people in wheelchairs. Ask the children to help find out about such events in your community. Make a list of these events and encourage the children to attend. If possible, your class may want to sponsor someone who is in a wheelchair for such an event. This could be done by making banners for people to hold along the race route as the person being sponsored passes by; by using magic numbers or special paint to make a shirt for him/her to wear in the event. A special *"cheer"* or *"chant"* could be created to yell along the race way for the person being sponsored.

3. Find someone who is in a wheelchair who would feel comfortable coming to the classroom and talking with the children about being in the wheelchair. Encourage the person to demonstrate how the wheelchair works and some of his/her experiences about being in a wheelchair. If possible, prior to the visit, obtain a wheelchair and crutches, on loan, from a hospital, ambulance

company, airport, or rehabilitation center. Then, under careful supervision and with the help of the visitor, allow the children to take turns using the equipment.

4.   Discuss with the children why they think people might need a wheelchair (for example, because they had an accident, were born without legs, or had a muscular disease or arthritis, and so on). Then discuss that some people use a wheelchair temporarily while for others it is a permanent part of their lives. Ask the children to think of people they have seen using wheelchairs and where the people were. Make a list of their responses and then discuss why the people might have been in a wheelchair. For example, often when people are discharged from the hospital, they are taken to their car in a wheelchair.

5.   Discuss the word *"contagious"* with the children, explaining that when doctors and scientists talk about something being contagious, it means you can *"catch it"* or *"get it"* from someone else. Sometimes it is difficult to know when you can *"catch something"* from someone and when you cannot. For example, if someone has a broken arm, can you *"catch it"* from them? Discuss several other diseases (measles, mumps, chicken pox) and non-diseases (spina bifida, HIV infection, asthma) to illustrate what you can and cannot *"catch"* from others. Ask the children to identify a time when they were sick with a contagious disease and to also identify a time when they or someone else had something wrong with them and it was not contagious.

Sensory Impairments
(Hearing and Visual)

Hearing Impairments

Children with hearing impairments may be deaf or hard of hearing. Children who are deaf demonstrate little or no hearing. Children who are hard of hearing process information from sound, usually with the assistance of a hearing aid.

Visual Impairments

Many people wear glasses or contact lenses and need to have their vision corrected or enhanced. These people differ from people with visual impairments in that, after they have their vision corrected, they see very well. Persons with visual impairments continue to have vision problems even after correction.

References

Aiello, B. (1988). *Business is looking up*. Frederick, MD: Twenty-first Century Books.

Arthur, C. (1979). *My sister's silent world*. Chicago, IL: Children's Press.

Aseltine, L., et al. (1992). *I'm deaf and it's okay*. Chicago, IL: Whitman.

Bergman, T. (1989). *Seeing in our special ways*. Milwaukee, WI: Gareth Stevens Children's Books.

Litchfield, A.B. (1992). *A button in her ear*. Chicago, IL: Whitman.

Litchfield, A.B. (1992). *A cane in her hand*. Chicago, IL: Whitman.

Litchfield, A.B. (1992). *Words in our hands*. Chicago, IL: Whitman.

MacLachlan, P. (1980). *Through grandpa's eyes*. New York: Harper & Collins.

St. George, J. (1992). *Dear Dr. Bell. . . your friend Helen Keller*. New York: Putnam.

Sullivan, M.B., Bourke, L., and Regan, S. (1992). *A show of hands: Say it in sign language*. New York: Harper & Collins.

Wild, M. (1992). *All the better to see you with*. Illustrated by P. Reynolds. New York: Checkerboard.

Activities

1. The National Association for Hearing and Speech Action, 10801 Rockville Pike, Rockville, MD 20852, 800-638-8255, will send a single copy of the manual alphabet (finger spelling) to you upon request. Duplicate this so that every child has a copy. Then ask them to learn to sign their names. Allow time to share. Encourage them to learn to sign each other's names.

2. Tell the children that sign language is another language just like Spanish, French, and German. Tell them that youngsters who are severely hearing impaired and deaf need to learn two languages—English and sign language. Just for fun, ask students to make up a new language. Tell them to write a paragraph in English and then translate the paragraph into their new language. Allow time to share.

3. There are many sign language books available, such as *Sesame Street Sign Language Fun*, produced by Children's Television Workshop (New York: Random House/Children's Television Workshop, 1980), 212-572-2646; *Words in Our Hands*, by Ada B. Litchfield (Chicago: Albert Whitman & Co., 1980), 312-647-1355; *Homemade ABC: A Manual Alphabet*, by Linda Bourke (Reading, MA: Addison-Wesley Publishing Co., Inc., 1981), 617-944-3700; *Basic Sign Communication*, by William J. Newall, National Association of the Deaf. Using the information provided in these books, teach the children some sign language for simple words that are frequently used, such as *good morning, goodbye, walk, run, stand, sit,* and the days of the week. Once signs are introduced, use them over and over in the daily activities. Keep a list of *"Sign Language Words We Know"* on the bulletin board or chalkboard. Review the list daily.

4. Invite someone to come to the class to talk with the children in sign language.

Cognitively Challenged Students
(Learning Disabilities and Mental Retardation)

Learning Disabled

Children with learning disabilities are sometimes thought of as being lazy, not as smart as other children, not being able to learn, and so on. None of this is necessarily true. Learning disabled students have an I.Q. within the average range but do not perform as well as other children their age.

References

Aiello, B. and Shulman, J. (1988). *Secrets aren't always for keeps*. Illustrated by Loel Barr. Frederick, MD: Twenty-first Century Books.

Janover, C. (1988). *Josh, a boy with dyslexia*. Illustrated by Edward Epstein. Burlington, VT: Waterfront Books.

Mentally Retarded

Children identified as being mentally retarded do have a lower than normal I.Q. (below 75). They do not get along independently, socially, or academically as well as other children their ages. Down's Syndrome is included in this category.

Help students to gain a better understanding and acceptance of children who are either learning disabled or mentally retarded by reading the suggested books and completing the activities that follow.

References

Amenta, C.A. III (1992). *Russell is extra special: A book about autism for children.* Pasadena, CA: Magination.

Berkus, C.W. (1991). *Charlsie's Chuckle.* Rockville, MD: Woodbine House.

Dunn, K.B. and Dunn, A.B. (1993). *Trouble with school.* Rockville, MD: Woodbine House.

Fleming, V. (1993). *Be good to Eddie Lee.* Illustrated by Floyd Cooper. New York: Putnam.

Gehret, J. (1990). *The don't give up kid.* Fairport, NY: Verbal Images Press.

Kroll, V.L. (1992). *My sister, then and now.* Minneapolis, MN: Carolrhoda.

Litchfield, A.B. (1992). *Making room for Uncle Joe.* Chicago, IL: Whitman.

O'Shaughnessy, E. (1992). *Somebody called me a retard today. . . and my heart felt sad.* New York: Walker.

Rabe, B. (1992). *Where Chimpy?* Chicago, IL: Whitman.

Rosenberg, M.B. (1983). *My friend Leslie.* New York: Lothrop, Lee and Shepard.

Activities

1. Introduce the books *Secrets Aren't Always for Keeps* by Barbara Aiello or *Josh, a Boy with Dyslexia* by Caroline Janover. Both books have questions about learning disabilities at the end. Read these questions and allow time for the children to answer them, based on their knowledge of learning disabilities. Then read the answers provided in the book. Allow time for discussion.

2. Barbara Aiello, author of *Secrets Aren't Always for Keeps,* has founded The Kids on the Block puppet program that was formed to introduce young audiences to the topic of children with disabilities. Her puppets have appeared in all 50 states and throughout the world. As a group, request more information about this program and a listing of her books by writing to The Kids on the Block, 9385-C Gerwig Lane, Columbia, Maryland 21046 or by calling 800-368-KIDS.

3. To find out more about learning disabilities, help the class write letters requesting information from the following organizations:

Association for Children and Adults with Learning Disabilities
4156 Library Road
Pittsburgh, PA 15234

Foundation for Children with Learning Disabilities
99 Park Avenue
New York, NY 10016

4.   There is an activity on page 93 in the book *Josh, a Boy with Dyslexia* by Caroline Janover entitled "What Does It Feel Like to Be Learning Disabled?" The activity involves the children standing in front of a mirror, placing a piece of paper against their foreheads, looking in the mirror, and then writing a word. As a group, do the activity, look at the word, discuss how the word looks and the difficulties one would have in reading the word. Point out that this is the way many learning disabled children see the words they read and write.

Behavior Disorders/Emotional Disturbances

Children who have behavior disorders and/or emotional disturbances are easy to recognize but difficult to define. We all know children who demonstrate behavior difficulties in particular settings or with particular people. The degree and the intensity of the behavior is the most important thing to consider. Hopefully, children will gain an insight into their own behaviors as well as that of others as they read the following books and complete the suggested activities.

References

Bosch, C. (1993). *Bully on the bus: A decision is yours book.* Illustrated by Rebekah Strecher. Burlington, VT: Waterfront Books.

Carlson, N. (1983). *Loudmouth George and the big race.* Minneapolis, MN: Carolrhoda Books.

Dunbar, J. (1988). *A cake for Barney.* Illustrated by Emilie Book. New York: Watts.

Gehret, J. (1991). *Eagle eye: A child's view of Attention Deficit Disorder.* Illustrated by Susan Covert. Fairport, NY: Verbal Images Press.

Leverich, K. (1992). *Hillary and the troublemakers.* New York: Greenwillow.

Lopshire, R. (1986). *I want to be somebody new.* New York: Random House.

Moss, M. (1992). *But not Kate.* New York: Lothrop, Lee, & Shephard.

Quackenbush, R.M. (1983). *I don't want to go, I don't know how to act.* New York: Lippincott.

Activities

1.   Discuss with the children how everyone misbehaves at one time or another. Ask the children to describe orally, or in written form, a time when they misbehaved. Ask them to include consequences, how they felt, why they did it, etc.

2.   Ask the children to dictate misbehaviors to you as you write them on the chalkboard. For example, fighting, yelling, cheating, lying, stealing, etc. After the list is completed, divide the children into groups of 4 or 5 and ask them to number 1 through 10, the ten most serious behaviors, with 1 being the most serious. After the groups have had time to prioritize the misbehaviors, get back into a large group and try to come up with agreement about ranking the most serious to the least serious behaviors.

3.   Read and/or make available some of the books recommended for this unit. After the children have had an opportunity to become familiar with the books, discuss the behaviors of the main characters in the books.

4.   Ask the children to illustrate what they think misbehavior looks like. Allow time to share.

Primary Unit: The Caldecott Award

Theme: THE CALDECOTT AWARD

Focus: Students will become aware of the diversity of artistic media used to illustrate children's books and become familiar with those illustrators whose books have been awarded the Caldecott Award for the most distinguished picture book published in the United States.

Objectives: Upon completion of this thematic unit, students will be able to:

1. Recognize the work of well-known award-winning illustrators of picture books.

2. Identify various artistic media used to illustrate picture books.

3. Evaluate picture books based upon certain criteria.

4. Use various artistic media to create their own illustrations.

Initiating Activity: Show students the covers of several books that have been awarded the Caldecott for outstanding illustrations. Ask students to study the covers to see what they have in common. (The answer is the Caldecott Medal.) Explain that each of these books was awarded the Caldecott Medal, which is presented each year by a special awards committee to the most distinguished picture book for children published in America. After discussing the logo on the actual medal, provide students with materials and ribbon to design their own Caldecott Medal. They will have the opportunity to bestow their creations on their selection for the Caldecott Award (see Culminating Activity).

General Activities:

1. Read aloud several Caldecott Medal or Honor books whose illustrations are created using a similar media, such as collage, woodcuts, watercolors, pen and ink, chalk, and so forth. Ask your school's art teacher or a local artist to demonstrate this same technique to your students and give them the opportunity to experiment with the selected media.

2. Read aloud several Caldecott Medal or Honor books that were illustrated by the same artist. Create a classroom display that includes a picture of the illustrator and a selection of books he or she illustrated. Help students identify the artistic techniques used in the different books.

3. Share a Caldecott Medal book with children by having them interpret the story from the pictures alone. Record their predictions and then, after reading the story, compare their versions to the actual text. Discuss how the illustrations of a picture book alone should be able to tell the story as well as create a mood.

4. Allow children to select a favorite Caldecott Medal or Honor book. Rewrite the text on large chart paper and give each group of students a different page to illustrate. Bind the pages together to form a big book that can be part of the class library.

5. Have students create a large collage mural, "CELEBRATING THE CALDECOTTS." For each Caldecott Medal and Honor book they have read, have students add pictures and objects to the mural that represents the book in some way.

6. After students have been involved in reading many of the books that have been awarded the Caldecott Medal, poll the class and select a favorite illustrator. Have students decorate the class door with student-made book jackets for the various children's books this person has illustrated.

7. Have students select their favorite Caldecott Medal or Honor book and recreate one of the pictures in the book (using the same media whenever possible). Create a classroom art gallery in which each picture is signed and matted and labeled with the name of the Caldecott book, author, and illustrator that inspired the student's picture.

8. Share the work of a Caldecott-winning illustrator. With students, brainstorm a list of adjectives that describes the artist's work. Divide students into groups and have each group select a Caldecott-winning illustrator and create a similar list. Have students use their list to create a commercial to promote one or more of this artist's picture book(s). Have them present their commercials in other classrooms to familiarize children with the artist and his or her work.

9. Select a Caldecott Medal or Honor book, read it aloud to students without showing the pictures, and have them imagine the illustrations. Next, reread the book and share the illustrations. Ask students, "How did the pictures in your mind compare with the pictures in the story?" "In what ways did the illustrations add to your enjoyment of the story?"

10. Introduce students to the work of famous artists of the past (for example, Degas, Rembrandt, Picasso, or Renoir) through series such as those published by HarperCollins and Rizzoli's Weekend with the Artist Series. In pairs, ask students to select a famous artist of the past whose work reminds them in some way of the work of one of the Caldecott illustrators. Have them create a conversation between the two artists in which they talk about their work. Ask students to present the conversation to the rest of the class and share examples of their work.

11. Have students create a slide show of Caldecott winners by taking pictures of the covers of each book and having them developed into slides. Each pair of students can be assigned one of the books and write a brief script telling a little about the book and its illustrations. Arrange the slides in chronological order (by the year the Caldecott was won) and have students record their scripts in the same order. To indicate that the slides should be advanced, have students ring a bell or create a special sound effect. You may also have students select background music for their recording.

Discussion Questions:

1. Why was the Caldecott Award established? (To honor the work of outstanding illustrators of children's books.)

2. Who was the Caldecott Award named for? (Randolph Caldecott, a prominent English illustrator of children's books, who lived from 1846 to 1886.)

3. What, in your opinion, is the most important thing illustrations for children's books must do?

4. Who is your favorite Caldecott-winning illustrator? Why?

5. Of the different media used to create the illustrations of picture books, which is your favorite? Why?

Literature Related Activities

(Note: Each of the Caldecott Award-winning books included in this section represents a different form of artistic media.)

Title: *The Snowy Day*

Genre: Picture Book—realistic fiction

Author: Ezra Jack Keats

Illustrator: Ezra Jack Keats (collage)

Bibliographic Information: Viking, New York, 1962

Summary: Readers will share in a young boy's adventures in the snow and celebrate the wonders of childhood.

Interest Level: Grades K –3.

1. Pre-Reading Activity:

    Have children imagine all the things they would do on a snowy day. Have each of them select a favorite snow activity, illustrate it, and give the picture a creative caption.

2. Learning Activities:

    a. Have students create a word cluster for the word "snow." Read them several poems on the subject of snow (consult the subject indexes of poetry anthologies) and use a favorite poem as a model for student's to create their own poem about snow. Bind their poetry into a book and include the illustrations from the pre-reading activity.

    b. Involve students in miming different activities they can do in the snow. Allow others in the class to guess what activity is being mimed (for example, riding a sled, making snowballs, having a snowball fight, building a snowman, etc.).

    c. Share other books whose illustrations are made from collage, such as Eric Carle's *The Very Hungry Caterpillar*, *The Very Busy Spider* and *The Very Quiet Cricket*; Leo Lionni's *Inch by Inch*; Mem Fox's *Hattie and the Fox*; or Marcia Brown's *Shadow*. Involve students in comparing the collages in these books with the collages in *The Snowy Day*.

    d. Involve students in a discussion of seasons. Begin by discussing winter. Ask those who have experienced snow to tell what they liked and didn't like about it. For those who have never experienced snow, ask them to imagine what snow would be like. Discuss activities students would do in the winter and in the snow. Continue the discussion, including the other seasons. Have students create a collage to illustrate their adventures during their favorite season.

    e. Read aloud to students other books by Ezra Keats, such as *Peter's Chair*, *Goggles*, *A Letter to Amy*, *Hi Cat!*, and *Pet Show!* In groups, have students reenact their favorite Keats book using some type of puppetry, such as bag puppets, finger puppets, stick puppets, etc.

f. Involve students in a discussion of snow and how it is formed. Read aloud Shel Silverstein's poem "Snowman" (from *Where the Sidewalk Ends*), which tells about a snowman on the first day of spring whose wish is to see July. Have them create snowflakes from white paper and have them list their favorite snow activity on their snowflake. After sharing their flakes, display their work on a "Snowy Day" bulletin board.

3. Discussion Questions

a. Of all Peter's adventures in the snow, which one would you enjoy most? What things have you done in the snow that Peter didn't do?

b. What happened to Peter's snowball? (It melted.) What could he have done to prevent it from melting? (Put it in the freezer.)

c. Why do you think the author had Peter playing alone in the snow the first day, rather than with a friend?

d. The art form in *The Snowy Day* is called collage. Describe this artistic media. (Collage is made by cutting different kinds of materials—newspaper clippings, patterned wall-paper, fabric, etc.—and combining them to form an illustration.)

Title:	*Drummer Hoff*
Genre:	Picture Book—traditional literature (cumulative tale)
Author:	Adapted by Barbara Emberley
Illustrator:	Ed Emberley (woodcuts)
Bibliographic Information:	Simon and Schuster, New York, 1967
Summary:	Each member of a group of soldiers has a specific role in firing a cannon. This cumulative tale works backward from the firing of the cannon, adding one detail at a time.
Interest Level:	Grades K–3.

---

1. Pre-Reading Activity:

Involve students in making predictions about the subject matter of *Drummer Hoff* based on the title and cover illustration alone. List their predictions and after reading the story allow them to see how accurate their predictions were.

2. Learning Activities:

a. After reading this cumulative tale several times, write the story events on sentence strips. Have students, in groups, sequence the strips and read their versions aloud.

b. Have students create drums made from various materials. As you read the tale aloud, have students create a beat to accompany the reading.

c. Have students create an accordion book to retell the tale. (See Figure 1.) Each group of students should be responsible for reproducing one of the pages of the tale for placement in the accordion book. To create an accordion book, fold a large piece of shelf paper accordion-style to form the pages. To make a cover, paste or staple cardboard to the first and last pages. Punch holes in the sides of the covers and fasten with ribbon to close the book.

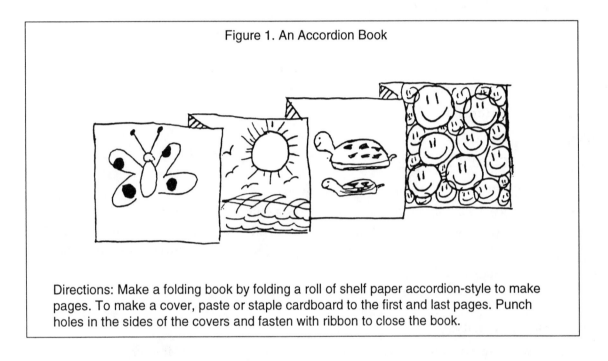

Figure 1. An Accordion Book

Directions: Make a folding book by folding a roll of shelf paper accordion-style to make pages. To make a cover, paste or staple cardboard to the first and last pages. Punch holes in the sides of the covers and fasten with ribbon to close the book.

d. Ask students to select another subject that requires several steps, such as making a peanut butter and jelly sandwich. Using *Drummer Hoff* as a model, have students create a cumulative tale explaining how the sandwich is made. Then, following the steps, provide the ingredients and let students make their sandwiches—and eat them!

e. Invite an art teacher to demonstrate the art of using woodcuts. Involve the class in using this art form.

f. Point out to students that only three basic colors were used to create the illustrations for *Drummer Hoff*—red, blue, and yellow. Ask students what colors were created from combining these colors. Involve students in experimenting with various basic primary colors to form secondary colors such as green, purple, orange, and pink. Have students create a color wheel that explains what colors can be combined to form additional colors.

g. *Drummer Hoff* has been made into a sound filmstrip by Weston Woods. Try to obtain a copy of this filmstrip and show it to students.

3. Discussion Questions

   a. Using the picture clues, where do you think the tale takes place? What clues helped you decide its location?

   b. What were Drummer Hoff and his fellow soldiers working together to do? (Fire a cannon.)

   c. Whose job was most important? Why? (Encourage students to understand the importance of teamwork and the fact that each person on the team is equally important.)

   d. Why do you think this book was selected to receive the Caldecott Medal? Do you agree or disagree with the choice?

Title: *Black and White*

Genre: Picture Book

Author: David Macaulay

Illustrator: David Macaulay

Bibliographic Information: Houghton Mifflin, Boston, 1990

Summary: *Black and White* is actually four stories in one, each created using a different media, including watercolors, torn paper, sepia, and pen and ink. The book is like a puzzle and readers must interpret each of the stories and seek a connection among them.

Interest Level: Grades 2–6.

---

1. Pre-Reading Activity:

   Read the warning that appears on the title page of the book. Discuss their interpretations of the warning.

2. Learning Activities:

   a. Have students divide a large piece of poster paper into four squares. In each square, have them write the name of one of the stories in *Black and White*. Next, have them write a brief summary of the story and draw an illustration to represent it.

   b. Divide the class into groups of four or five. Have each group create their own interpretation of *Black and White* by combining the four stories into one. Have each group present their interpretation in the form of a dramatic skit, using masks, puppetry, flannel board characters, or other artistic forms.

   c. Many have compared *Black and White* to a jigsaw puzzle. Have students create a jigsaw puzzle representing one of the illustrations in *Black and White*. This can be done using the following steps:

      1. Have students select a favorite illustration and create his or her own version of it. Somewhere on the picture, ask students to write the name of the story from which the picture came.

2. Glue the picture to a thin piece of cardboard and laminate.

3. Have students draw puzzle piece designs over the puzzle and cut it out accordingly.

Allow time for students to put each others' puzzles together.

d. Encourage students to create their own books modeled after *Black and White*. Students, in groups of six, can brainstorm three different scenarios that can be combined in some way. Pairs can work together on one of the scenarios, being certain to include clues and pictures from the other stories. When the pages are completed, laminate and bind them.

e. Encourage students to read other books by David Macaulay (all published by Houghton Mifflin) such as *The Way Things Work* (1988); *Why the Chicken Crossed the Road* (1987); *Castle* (1977); *Cathedral: The Story of its Construction* (1974); *Mill* (1983); *Pyramid* (1975); and *Underground* (1976). Involve students in developing an interesting and creative activity based on one of the books.

3. Discussion Questions

a. Why do you believe Macaulay gave the book the title, *Black and White*. Of all the reasons you can think of, which do you think is the most probable?

b. *Black and White* is quite different from other picture books. Explain the ways in which it differs. (Most picture books are read from left to right; most books describe a story in sequence; most books have the dedication at the front of the book; the pictures in most books are done in the same style and use the same media throughout the book; and so forth.)

c. Of the four stories included in the book, which is your favorite? Why? Which is your least favorite? Explain.

d. Some people have compared reading *Black and White* to flipping television stations. Do you agree or disagree? What other comparison can you make?

e. Do you believe *Black and White* is really four separate stories or are they simply one story told in an unusual way? Explain.

Title:	*Tuesday*
Genre:	Picture Book—fantasy
Author:	David Wiesner
Illustrator:	David Wiesner (watercolors)
Bibliographic Information:	Clarion, New York, 1991
Summary:	The incredible adventures of a group of frogs, one Tuesday evening, somewhere in the U.S.A.
Interest Level:	Grades K–6.

1. Pre-Reading Activity:

    Explain to students that the idea for writing *Tuesday* came to Wiesner from a cover he created for the March 1989 issue of *Cricket Magazine*. In the issue (locate and share the issue, if possible) there were many stories and pictures about frogs. For inspiration, he looked through some *National Geographic* magazines for pictures of frogs. Have students begin a frog collection by bringing in as many pictures of frogs as they can find. Have them create huge lily pads and cover them with pictures from the frog collection and with words and phrases that they would use to describe frogs.

2. Learning Activities:

    a. Encourage groups of children to create words to accompany this wordless picture book. Have them tape their version on a cassette and use a specific sound to cue the reader to turn the page.

    b. Have students create a mural sequel to the book, entitled *Next Tuesday*, in which pigs fly. Ask each student to imagine an adventure for the pigs and recreate it using watercolors, the same media used in *Tuesday*.

    c. Have students create a special news broadcast in which they tell about the incredible events of Tuesday as if they were actually happening. Encourage them to be creative—they can even interview several of the frogs and other characters from the story.

    d. Have students research frogs and find five facts about them. Have them create an informational book about frogs using illustrations from the book (photocopy or have students recreate pages such as the one showing the frogs leaping, diving, and sitting on the lily pads) to accompany the facts they have written.

3. Discussion Questions

    a. What did Wiesner do to make the events in the story seem almost believable? (He gave the precise times of the frogs' adventure and used pictures that seemed almost like photographs.)

    b. Imagine that you were the inspector in the story who was trying to figure out what had happened. What clues did he find? What other possible solutions could you come up with?

    c. Which illustrations show frogs doing things that frogs are generally expected to do?

    d. Which picture in the book is your favorite? Explain why.

Culminating Activity: "The One That Got Away." Students have been spending a good deal of time involved with books that have been named Caldecott winners or Honor books. With students, create a list of criteria that they think illustrations must meet to be considered outstanding. Provide students with recently published picture books that have not been awarded the Caldecott. Ask each student to select a book that he or she feels should have been awarded the Caldecott, and have each nominate the book by filling in the form on page 53. Based on the information they listed on the nomination form, have each create and present a short persuasive speech explaining to classmates the reasons the book deserves special recognition for its illustrations. Have each student award the book the medal that he or she created in the Initiating Activity and display the books, nomination forms, and awards for several days. At the end of a specific period of time, have the class vote for the most outstanding picture book from those nominated. Involve the class in writing a letter to the illustrator (in care of the publisher) to tell him or her of the class's interest in and enthusiasm for the book.

Caldecott Nomination Form

Title: _____

Illustrator: _____

Author: _____

Publisher: _____ Date of Publication: _____

In 20 words or less, explain why you believe this book should win an award for its illustrations.

_____

_____

_____

_____

_____

_____

In one word or phrase, describe the illustrations.

_____

Student's Name _____ Date _____

Supplemental Literature

The following is a comprehensive list of all those books that have been named Caldecott Medal Winners and Caldecott Honor Books, from the establishment of the Caldecott Award in 1938 until 1993.

1938   *Animals of the Bible* by Helen Dean Fish, illustrated by Dorothy P. Lathrop, Lippincott

Honor Books: *Seven Simeons* by Boris Artzybasheff, Viking; *Four and Twenty Blackbirds* by Helen Dean Fish, illustrated by Robert Lawson, Stokes

1939   *Mei Li* by Thomas Handforth, Doubleday

Honor Books: *The Forest Pool* by Laura Adams Armer, Longmans; *Wee Gillis* by Munro Leaf, illustrated by Robert Lawson, Viking; *Snow White and the Seven Dwarfs* by Wanda Gág, Coward; *Barkis* by Clare Newberry, Harper; *Andy and the Lion* by James Daugherty, Viking

1940   *Abraham Lincoln* by Ingri and Edgar Parin D'Aulaire, Doubleday

Honor Books: *Cock-A-Doodle Doo...* by Berta and Elmer Hader, Macmillan; *Madeline* by Ludwig Bemelmans, Viking; *The Ageless Story* illustrated by Lauren Ford, Dodd

1941   *They Were Strong and Good* by Robert Lawson, Viking

Honor Book: *April's Kittens* by Clare Newberry, Harper

1942   *Make Way for Ducklings* by Robert McCloskey, Viking

Honor Books: *An American ABC* by Maud and Miska Petersham, Macmillan; *In My Mother's House* by Ann Nolan Clark, illustrated by Velino Herrera, Viking; *Paddle-to-the-Sea* by Holling C. Holling, Houghton; *Nothing at All* by Wanda Gág, Coward.

1943   *The Little House* by Virginia Lee Burton, Houghton

Honor Books: *Dash and Dart* by Mary and Conrad Buff, Viking; *Marshmallow* by Clare Newberry, Harper

1944   *Many Moons* by James Thurber, illustrated by Louis Slobodkin, Harcourt

Honor Books: *Small Rain: Verses from the Bible* selected by Jessie Orton Jones, illustrated by Ellzabeth Orton Jones, Viking; *Pierre Pigeon* by Lee Kingman, illustrated by Arnold E. Bare, Houghton; *The Mighty Hunter* by Berta and Elmer Hader, Macmillan; *A Child's Good Night Book* by Margaret Wise Brown, illustrated by Jean Charlot, W. R Scott; *Good Luck Horse* by Chih-Yi Chan, illustrated by Plao Chan, Whittlesey

1945   *Prayer for a Child* by Rachel Field, illustrated by Ellzabeth Orton Jones, Macmillan

Honor Books: *Mother Goose* Illustrated by Tasha Tudor, Walck; *In the Forest* by Marie Hall Ets, Viking; *Yonie Wondernose* by Marguerite de Angeli, Doubleday; *The Christmas Anna Angel* by Ruth Sawyer, illustrated by Kate Seredy, Viking

1946   *The Rooster Crows...* (traditional Mother Goose) illustrated by Maud and Miska Petersham, Macmillan

Honor Books: *Little Lost Lamb* by Golden MacDonald, illustrated by Leonard Weisgard, Doubleday; *Sing Mother Goose* by Opal Wheeler, illustrated by Marjorie Torrey, Dutton; *My Mother Is the Most Beautiful Woman in the World* by Becky Reyher, illustrated by Ruth Gannett, Lothrop; *You Can Write Chinese* by Kurt Wiese, Viking

1947   *The Little Island* by Golden MacDonald, illustrated by Leonard Weisgard, Doubleday

Honor Books: *Rain Drop Splash* by Alvin Tresselt, illustrated by Leonard Weisgard, Lothrop; *Boats on the River* by Marjorie Flack, illustrated by Jay Hyde Barnum, Viking; *Timothy Turtle* by Al Graham, illustrated by Tony Palazzo, Viking; *Pedro, The Angel of Olvera Street* by Leo Politi, Scribner's; *Sing in Praise: A Collection of the Best Loved Hymns* by Opal Wheeler, illustrated by Marjorie Torrey, Dutton

1948   *White Snow, Bright Snow* by Alvin Tresselt, illustrated by Roger Duvoisin, Lothrop

Honor Books: *Stone Soup* by Marcia Brown, Scribner's; *McElligot's Pool* by Dr. Seuss, Random; *Bambino the Clown* by George Schreiber, Viking; *Roger and the Fox* by Lavinia Davis, illustrated by Hildegard Woodward, Doubleday; *Song of Robin Hood* edited by Anne Malcolmson, illustrated by Virginia Lee Burton, Houghton

1949   *The Big Snow* by Berta and Elmer Hader, Macmillan

Honor Books: *Blueberries for Sal* by Robert McCloskey, Viking; *All Around the Town* by Phyllis McGinley, illustrated by Helen Stone, Lippincott; *Juanita* by Leo Politi, Scribner's; *Fish in the Air* by Kurt Wiese, Viking

1950   *Song of the Swallows* by Leo Politi, Scribner's

Honor Books: *America's Ethan Allen* by Stewart Holbrook, illustrated by Lynd Ward, Houghton; *The Wild Birthday Cake* by Lavinia Davis, illustrated by Hildegard Woodward, Doubleday; *The Happy Day* by Ruth Krauss, illustrated by Marc Simont, Harper; *Bartholomew and the Oobleck* by Dr. Seuss, Random; *Henry Fisherman* by Marcia Brown, Scribner's

1951   *The Egg Tree* by Katherine Milhous, Scribner's

Honor Books: *Dick Whittington and His Cat* by Marcia Brown, Scribner's; *The Two Reds* by William Lipkind, illustrated by Nicholas Mordvinoff, Harcourt; *If I Ran the Zoo* by Dr. Seuss, Random; *The Most Wonderful Doll in the World* by Phyllis McGinley, illustrated by Helen Stone, Lippincott; *T-Bone, the Baby Sitter* by Clare Newberry, Harper

1952   *Finders Keepers* by William Lipkind, illustrated by Nicholas Mordvinoff, Harcourt

Honor Books: *Mr. T. W. Anthony Woo* by Marie Hall Ets, Viking; *Skipper John's Cook* by Marcia Brown, Scribner's; *All Falling Down* by Gene Zion, illustrated by Margaret Bloy Graham, Harper; *Bear Party* by William Pène du Bois, Viking; *Feather Mountain* by Elizabeth Olds, Houghton

1953   *The Biggest Bear* by Lynd Ward, Houghton

Honor Books: *Puss in Boots* by Charles Perrault, illustrated and translated by Marcia Brown, Scribner's; *One Morning in Maine* by Robert McCloskey, Viking; *Ape in a Cape* by Fritz Eichenberg, Harcourt; *The Storm Book* by Charlotte Zolotow, illustrated by Margaret Bloy Graham, Harper; *Five Little Monkeys* by Juliet Kepes, Houghton

1954   *Madeline's Rescue* by Ludwig Bemelmans, Viking

Honor Books: *Journey Cake, Ho!* by Ruth Sawyer, illustrated by Robert McCloskey, Viking; *When Will the World Be Mine?* by Miriam Schlein, illustrated by Jean Charlot, W. R. Scott; *The Steadfast Tin Soldier* by Hans Christian Andersen, illustrated by Marcia Brown, Scribner's; *A Very Special House* by Ruth Krauss, illustrated by Maurice Sendak, Harper; *Green Eyes* by A. Birnbaum, Capitol

1955   *Cinderella, or the Little Glass Slipper* by Charles Perrault, translated and illustrated by Marcia Brown, Scribner's

Honor Books: *Books of Nursery and Mother Goose Rhymes*, illustrated by Marguerite de Angeli, Doubleday; *Wheel on the Chimney* by Margaret Wise Brown, illustrated by Tibor Gergely, Lippincott; *The Thanksgiving Story* by Alice Dalgliesh, illustrated by Helen Sewell, Scribner's

1956   *Frog Went A-Courtin'*, edited by John Langstaff, illustrated by Feodor Rojankovsky, Harcourt

Honor Books: *Play with Me* by Marie Hall Ets, Viking; *Crow Boy* by Taro Yashima, Viking

1957   *A Tree Is Nice* by Janice May Udry, illustrated by Marc Simont, Harper

Honor Books: *Mr. Penny's Race Horse* by Marie Hall Ets, Viking; *1 Is One* by Tasha Tudor, Walck; *Anatole* by Eve Titus, illustrated by Paul Galdone, McGraw; *Gillespie and the Guards* by Benjamin Elkin, illustrated by James Daugherty, Viking; *Lion* by William Pène du Bois, Viking

1958   *Time of Wonder* by Robert McCloskey, Viking

Honor Books: *Fly High, Fly Low* by Don Freeman, Viking; *Anatole and the Cat* by Eve Titus, illustrated by Paul Galdone, McGraw

1959   *Chanticleer and the Fox*, adapted from Chaucer and illustrated by Barbara Cooney, T. Crowell

Honor Books: *The House That Jack Built* by Antonio Frasconi, Harcourt; *What Do You Say, Dear?* by Sesyle Joslin, illustrated by Maurice Sendak, W. R. Scott; *Umbrella* by Taro Yashima, Viking

1960   *Nine Days to Christmas* by Marie Hall Ets and Aurora Labastida, illustrated by Marie Hall Ets, Viking

Honor Books: *Houses from the Sea* by Alice E. Goudey, illustrated by Adrienne Adams, Scribner's; *The Moon Jumpers* by Janice May Udry, illustrated by Maurice Sendak, Harper

1961   *Baboushka and the Three Kings* by Ruth Robbins, illustrated by Nicholas Sidjakov, Parnassus

Honor Book: *Inch by Inch* by Leo Lionni, Obolensky

1962   *Once a Mouse...* by Marcia Brown, Scribner's

Honor Books: *The Fox Went Out on a Chilly Night* by Peter Spier, Doubleday; *Little Bear's Visit* by Else Holmelund Minarik, illustrated by Maurice Sendak, Harper; *The Day We Saw the Sun Come Up* by Alice E. Goudey, illustrated by Adrienne Adams, Scribner's

1963   *The Snowy Day* by Ezra Jack Keats, Viking

Honor Books: *The Sun Is a Golden Earring* by Natalia M. Belting, illustrated by Bernarda Bryson, Holt; *Mr. Rabbit and the Lovely Present* by Charlotte Zolotow, illustrated by Maurice Sendak, Harper

1964   *Where the Wild Things Are* by Maurice Sendak, Harper & Row

Honor Books: *All in the Morning Early* by Sorche Nic Leodhas, illustrated by Evaline Ness, Holt, Rinehart & Winston; *Mother Goose and Nursery Rhymes* by Philip Reed, Atheneum; *Swimmy* by Leo Lionni, Pantheon

1965   *May I Bring a Friend?* by Beatrice Schenk de Regniers, Atheneum

Honor Books: *A Pocketful of Cricket* by Rebecca Caudill, illustrated by Evaline Ness, Holt, Rinehart & Winston; *Rain Makes Applesauce* by Julian Scheer, illustrated by Marvin Bileck, Holiday; *The Wave* by Margaret Hodges, illustrated by Blair Lent, Houghton Mifflin

1966   *Always Room for One More* by Sorche Nic Leodhas, illustrated by Nonny Hogrogian, Holt, Rinehart & Winston

Honor Books: *Hide and Seek Fog* by Alvin Tresselt, illustrated by Roger Duvoisin, Lothrop, Lee

& Shepard; *Just Me* by Marie Hall Ets, Viking; *Tom Tit Tot* edited by Joseph Jacobs, illustrated by Evaline Ness, Scribner's

1967   *Sam, Bangs & Moonshine* by Evaline Ness, Holt, Rinehart & Winston

Honor Book: *One Wide River to Cross* by Barbara Emberley, illustrated by Ed Emberley, Prentice-Hall

1968   *Drummer Hoff* by Barbara Emberley, illustrated by Ed Emberley, Prentice-Hall

Honor Books: *Frederick* by Leo Lionni, Pantheon; *Seashore Story* by Taro Yashima, Viking; *The Emperor and the Kite* by Jane Yolen, illustrated by Ed Young, Harcourt Brace Jovanovich

1969   *The Fool of the World and the Flying Ship* by Arthur Ransome, illustrated by Uri Shulevitz, Farrar, Straus & Giroux

Honor Book: *Why the Sun and the Moon Live in the Sky: An African Folktale* by Elphinstone Dayrell, illustrated by Blair Lent, Houghton Mifflin

1970   *Sylvester and the Magic Pebble* by William Steig, Windmill/Simon & Schuster

Honor Books: *Alexander and the Wind-Up Mouse* by Leo Lionni, Pantheon; *Goggles!* Ezra Jack Keats, Macmillan; *The Judge: An Untrue Tale* by Harve Zemach, illustrated by Margot Zemach, Farrar, Straus & Giroux; *Pop Corn & Ma Goodness* by Edna Mitchell Preston, illustrated by Robert Andrew Parker, Viking; *Thy Friend, Obadiah* by Brinton Turkle, Viking

1971   *A Story, A Story* by Gail E. Haley, Atheneum

Honor Books: *The Angry Moon* by William Sleaton, illustrated by Blair Lent, Atlantic-Little; *Frog and Toad Are Friends* by Arnold Lobel, Harper & Row; *In the Night Kitchen* by Maurice Sendak, Harper & Row

1972   *One Fine Day* by Nonny A. Hogrogian, Macmillan

Honor Books: *Hildilid's Night* by Cheli Duran Ryan, illustrated by Arnold Lobel, Macmillan; *If All the Seas Were One Sea* by Janina Domanska, Macmillan; *Moja Means One: Swahili Counting Book* by Muriel Feelings, illustrated by Tom Feelings, Dial

1973   *The Funny Little Woman* by Arlen Mosel, illustrated by Blair Lent, E. P. Dutton

Honor Books: *Hosie's Alphabet* by Hosea, Tobias, and Lisa Baskin, illustrated by Leonard Baskin, Viking; *Snow White and the Seven Dwarfs*, translated by Randall Jarrell from The Brothers Grimm, illustrated by Nancy Ekholm Burkert, Farrar, Straus & Giroux; *When Clay Sings* by Byrd Baylor, illustrated by Tom Bahti, Scribner's

1974   *Duffy and the Devil* by Harve and Margot Zemach, Farrar, Straus & Giroux

Honor Books: *Cathedral: The Story of Its Construction* by David Macaulay, Houghton; *The Three Jovial Huntsmen* by Susan Jeffers, Bradbury

1975   *Arrow to the Sun* by Gerald McDermott, Viking

Honor Book: *Jambo Means Hello: A Swahili Alphabet Book* by Muriel Feelings, illustrated by Tom Feelings, Dial

1976   *Why Mosquitoes Buzz in People's Ears* by Verna Aardema, illustrated by Leo and Diane Dillon, Dial

Honor Books: *The Desert Is Theirs* by Byrd Baylor, illustrated by Peter Parnall, Scribner's; *Strega Nona* by Tomie de Paola, Prentice-Hall

1977   *Ashanti to Zulu* by Margaret Musgrove, illustrated by Leo and Diane Dillon, Dial

Honor Books: *The Amazing Bone* by William Steig, Farrar, Straus & Giroux; *The Contest* by Nonny Hogrogian, Greenwillow; *Fish for Supper* by M. B. Goffstein, Dial; *The Golem: A Jewish Legend* by Beverly Brodsky McDermott, Lippincott; *Hawk, I'm Your Brother* by Byrd Baylor, illustrated by Peter Parnall, Scribner's

1978   *Noah's Ark: The Story of the Flood* by Peter Spier, Doubleday

Honor Books: *Castle* by David Macaulay, Houghton; *It Could Always Be Worse* by Margot Zemach, Farrar, Straus & Giroux

1979   *The Girl Who Loved Wild Horses* by Paul Goble, Bradbury

Honor Books: *Freight Train* by Donald Crews, Greenwillow; *The Way to Start a Day* by Byrd Baylor, illustrated by Peter Parnall, Scribner's

1980   *Ox-Cart Man* by Donald Hall, illustrated by Barbara Cooney, Viking

Honor Books: *Ben's Trumpet* by Rachel Isadora, Greenwillow; *The Garden of Abdul Gasazi* by Chris Van Allsburg, Houghton; *The Treasure* by Uri Shulevitz, Farrar, Straus & Giroux

1981   *Fables* by Arnold Lobel, Harper & Row

Honor Books: *The Bremen-Town Musicians* by Ilse Plume, Doubleday; *The Grey Lady and the Strawberry Snatcher* by Molly Bang, Four Winds; *Mice Twice* by Joseph Low, Atheneum; *Truck* by Donald Crews, Greenwillow

1982   *Jumanji* by Chris Van Allsburg, Houghton Mifflin

Honor Books: *On Market Street* by Arnold Lobel, illustrated by Anita Lobel, Greenwillow; *Outside over There* by Maurice Sendak, Harper & Row; *A Visit to William Blake's Inn: Poems for Innocent and Experienced Travelers* by Nancy Willard, illustrated by Alice and Martin Provensen, Harcourt; *Where the Buffaloes Begin* by Olaf Baker, illustrated by Stephen Gammell, Warne

1983   *Shadow* by Blaise Cendrars, translated and illustrated by Marcia Brown, Scrlbner's

Honor Books: *A Chair for My Mother* by Vera B. Williams, Greenwillow; *When I Was Young in the Mountains* by Cynthia Rylant, illustrated by Diane Goode, E. P. Dutton

1984   *The Glorious Flight Across the Channel with Louis Bleriot* by Alice and Martin Provensen, Viking

Honor Books: *Little Red Riding Hood* by Trina Schart Hyman, Holiday; *Ten, Nine, Eight* by Molly Bang, Greenwillow

1985   *Saint George and the Dragon* by Margaret Hodges, illustrated by Trina Schart Hyman, Little, Brown

Honor Books: *Hansel and Gretel* by Rika Lesser, illustrated by Paul O. Zelinsky, Dodd, Mead; *Have You Seen My Duckling?* by Nancy Tafuri, Greenwillow; *The Story of Jumping Mouse* by John Steptoe, Lothrop, Lee & Shepard

1986   *The Polar Express* by Chris Van Allsburg, Houghton Mifflin

Honor Books: *King Bidgood's in the Bathtub* by Audrey Wood, Harcourt Brace Jovanovich; *The Relatives Came* by Cynthia Rylant, Bradbury

1987   *Hey, Al* by Arthur Yorinks, illustrated by Richard Egielski, Farrar, Straus & Giroux

Honor Books: *Alphabatics* by Suse MacDonald, Bradbury; *Rumplestiltskin* by Paul O. Zelinsky, E. P. Dutton; *The Village of Round and Square Houses* by Anne Grifalconi, Little, Brown

1988   *Owl Moon* by Jane Yolen, illustrated by John Schoenherr, Philomel

Honor Book: *Mufaro's Beautiful Daughters: An African Tale* by John Steptoe, Morrow

1989   *Song and Dance Man* by Karen Ackerman, illustrated by Stephen Gammell, Knopf

Honor Books: *The Boy of the Three Year Nap* by Dianne Snyder, illustrated by Allen Say, Houghton Mifflin; *Free Fall* by David Wiesner, Lothrop, Lee, & Shepard; *Goldilocks and the Three Bears* by James Marshall, Dial; *Mirandy and Brother Wind* by Patricia C. McKissack, illustrated by Jerry Pinkney, Knopf

1990   *Lon Po Po: A Red Riding Hood Story from China* by Ed Young, Putnam

Honor Books: *Bill Peet: An Autobiography,* written and illustrated by Bill Peet, Houghton Mifflin; *Color Zoo,* written and illustrated by Lois Ehlert, Harper & Row; *Hershel and the Hanukkah Goblins* by Eric A. Kimmel, illustrated by Trina Schart Hyman, Holiday; *The Talking Eggs* by Robert San Souci, illustrated by Jerry Pinkney, Doubleday

1991   *Black & White* by David Macaulay, Houghton Mifflin

Honor Books: *Puss in Boots* by Fred Marcellino, de Capua/Farrar; *"More, More, More" Said the Baby: 3 Love Stories* by Vera B. Williams, Greenwillow

1992   *Tuesday* by David Wiesner, Clarion Books

Honor Book: *Tar Beach* by Faith Ringgold, Crown Publishing

1993   *Seven Blind Mice* by Ed Young, Philomel Books

Honor Books: *The Stinky Cheese Man and Other Fairly Stupid Tales* by Jon Scieszka, illustrated by Lane Smith, Viking; *Working Cotton* by Sherley Anne Williams, illustrated by Carole Byard, Harcourt Brace Jovanovich

MINI-THEMES

The following mini-themes focus on four outstanding illustrators of children's books, each of whom has been recognized for his or her achievements by being awarded the Caldecott Medal. Their styles are unique and distinctive and their efforts have created unforgettable characters and images that will remain with children long after one of their books has been read.

*   indicates that the book was a Caldecott Medal Winner.

†   indicates that the book was a Caldecott Honor Book.

Maurice Sendak

Both an author and an illustrator, Sendak's illustrations always reflect the story, portraying a myriad of emotions—from the solemn and sensitive to the comedic. He is especially loved by children, who instantly recognize his ferocious, yet lovable Wild Things. Sendak received the prestigious Hans Christian Andersen Medal in 1970, the first American artist to be so honored.

References

DeJong, M. (1953). *Hurry home, Candy*. Illustrated by M. Sendak. New York: Harper.

† Krauss, R. (1953). *A very special house*. Illustrated by M. Sendak. New York: Harper.

† Minarik, E. H. (1961). *Little bear's visit*. Illustrated by M. Sendak. New York: Harper.

Sendak, M. (1962). *Chicken soup with rice*. New York: Harper.

Sendak, M. (1967). *Higglety, pigglety, pop!* New York: Harper.

† Sendak, M. (1990). *In the night kitchen*. New York: Harper.

† Sendak, M. (1981). *Outside over there*. New York: Harper.

* Sendak, M. (1963). *Where the wild things are*. New York: Harper.

† Udry, J. (1959). *The moon jumpers*. Illustrated by M. Sendak. New York: Harper.

† Zolotow, C. (1962). *Mr. Rabbit and the lovely present*. Illustrated by M. Sendak. New York: Harper.

Activities

1. After reading many of Sendak's books to students, poll them to find out which book is their favorite and create a chart that reflects their choices. Involve students in a literature circle in which they discuss their reasons for their preference.

2. Maurice Sendak won the Hans Christian Andersen Medal in 1970, the first time an American artist was so honored. Read aloud several of Sendak's books and share the illustrations. Ask students why, of all the illustrators of children's books, they believe Sendak was awarded this important medal.

3. Have students select a favorite Sendak book and create a mobile to represent the story.

4. Involve students in a shared reading of *Where the Wild Things Are* (Caldecott Winner). Have students create their own wild things from clay, paint, and an assortment of yarns, buttons, etc. Have students give their wild thing a name and write a brief biography of this creation.

5. Encourage children to find additional biographical information about Maurice Sendak. Have them read about Sendak, find five interesting facts about him, put them on poster paper, and illustrate each fact with a character or scene from one of his books.

6. Involve students in reading various books illustrated by Sendak. Have students create a costume for their favorite Sendak character. Have a Maurice Sendak day in which children parade through the school dressed as their characters. After the parade, assign each student to a different room in the school where he or she can retell the Sendak story in which his or her character appears.

Ed Young

Born in Tientsin, China, Ed Young grew up in Shanghai and his heritage is beautifully reflected in his art. Young's versatility is evident in the variety of artistic media he uses, including Oriental papercut technique, rich pastels, and pencil drawings.

References

Hearne, Lafacadio. (1989). *The voice of the great bell*. Adapted by M. Hodges. Illustrated by E. Young. Boston: Little, Brown.

Larrick, N. (1988). *Cats and Cats*. Illustrated by E. Young. New York: Philomel.

Louis, A. (1982). *Yeh-Shen: A Cinderella story from China*. Illustrated by E. Young. New York: Philomel.

Wolkstein, D. (1972). *8,000 stones: A Chinese folktale*. Illustrated by E. Young. New York: Doubleday.

Wolkstein, D. (1979). *White Wave: A Chinese tale*. Illustrated by E. Young. New York: Crowell.

Wyndham, R., compiler (1968). *Chinese Mother Goose rhymes*. Illustrated by E. Young. San Diego: Harcourt Brace Jovanovich.

† Yolen, J. (1967). *The emperor and the kite*. Illustrated by E. Young. San Diego: Harcourt Brace Jovanovich.

Yolen, J. (1972). *The girl who loved the wind*. Illustrated by E. Young. New York: Crowell.

* Young, E. (1989). *Lon Po Po: A Red Riding Hood story from China*. New York: Philomel.

* Young, E. (1992). *Three blind mice*. New York: Philomel.

Young, E. (1984). *The other bone*. New York: Harper.

Activities

1. Many of the books that Ed Young has illustrated are folktales. Of these, many are versions of some of the most popular tales children have grown up with, such as *Cinderella* and *Little Red Riding Hood*. Share various versions of these two tales, along with the versions illustrated by Ed Young. Involve students in a discussion of the two stories and the way the illustrations reflect the culture from which the story came. Have students select a favorite folktale and have them brainstorm ways they could transform it into a folktale from China. Encourage them to use their ideas to create a new version of the story.

2. Ed Young was born in Tientsin, China and grew up in Shanghai. Have students locate Tientsin and Shanghai on a map and research China to learn a little about Young's heritage. Have them create a mini-book (see directions on page 62) about China. On each of the eight pages, have students list one fact about China and illustrate the borders with pictures representative of the country and its rich culture.

Mini-Book Directions:

1. Begin with one 8 1/2 x 11" sheet of unlined paper or construction paper.

2. Fold in half, making folded creases tight.

3. Fold again.

4. Fold in half sideways.

5. Open to half a sheet (position #3). Hold with fold at the top and cut in the middle from fold to center.

6. Open sheet completely—there will be 8 folded boxes. Fold lengthwise.

7. Bring outer edges together to form the book. The book will contain 4 pages, front and back, for a total of 8 pages.

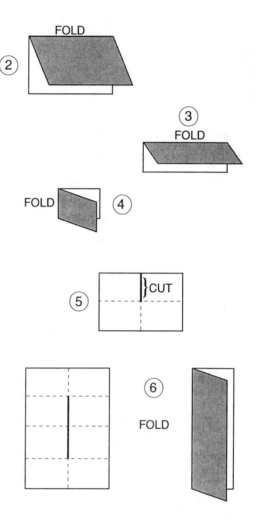

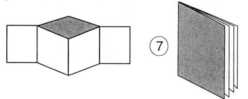

3. *The Other Bone* is a wordless picture book by Young. In groups, have students create a text for the story . Have each group select a different form of creative expression to tell their story (for example, puppetry, storytelling, story theater, flannel board, rap-song, etc.), and present it to the class.

4. From the various books Young has written and/or illustrated, students will form impressions about the Asian culture. Involve students in learning about the Chinese culture through many of their crafts, such as origami (the art of paper folding) and calligraphy (included in Young's illustrations for *Chinese Mother Goose Rhymes*). Invite guest speakers to demonstrate these art forms to students and have them experiment with them.

5. In *The Girl Who Loved the Wind*, the wind speaks verses to Danina, telling her about life outside the palace walls. Copy the various verses, writing each verse on a different sheet of large chart paper or onto pages of a blank big book. Make each group of students responsible for illustrating one page/verse with pictures, pieces of cloth and wallpaper, etc. that reflect the story and its setting. Students should also be encouraged to create a verse of their own as the last page of the newly formed big book.

Leo and Diane Dillon

The collaboration of these two artists results in a finished product created by what they term "the third artist." And, in their words, this artist, "comes up with things neither of us would have done." Coming from very different backgrounds, these two incredibly talented people met at the Parsons School of Design and were immediately captivated by each other's art.

References

* Aardema, V. (1975). *Why mosquitoes buzz in people's ears*. Illustrated by L. and D. Dillon. New York: Dial.

Aardema, V. (1973). *Behind the back of the mountain: Black folktales from Southern Africa*. Illustrated by L. and D. Dillon. New York: Dial.

Hamilton, V. (1985). *The people could fly*. Illustrated by L. and D. Dillon. New York: Knopf.

Mathis, S. B. (1976). *The hundred-penny box.* Illustrated by L. and D. Dillon. New York: Viking.

* Musgrove, M. (1976). *Ashanti to Zulu*. Illustrated by L. and D. Dillon. New York: Dial.

Price, L. (1990). *Aida*. Illustrated by L. and D. Dillon. San Diego: Harcourt.

Activities

1. The Dillons employ a variety of techniques and media in the different books they illustrate. Have students read a variety of books the Dillons have illustrated and select their favorite book, based on illustrations alone. Have students create a book jacket for the book, trying to reproduce one of the illustrations. On the jacket flaps, encourage them to tell a little bit about the story but mainly concentrate on writing about their impressions of the illustrations. Display the book jackets on a special bulletin board honoring the Dillons and their work.

2. Leo and Diane Dillon have worked on every illustration for their children's books together. In their words, "We each have our distinct styles and particular strengths, but... After a work is finished, not even we can be certain who did what. The third artist is a combination of the two of us and is different than either of us individually. ... It comes up with things neither of us would have done. (*Something About the Author*, Vol. 51, page 53.) Have students experiment with

collaborating with another student on a picture, first discussing media, subject, and style, and then passing the picture back and forth, with each student adding to it each time they receive it. Once the pictures have been completed, mat them and display.

3. Leo and Diane Dillon are the first, and so far only, artists to have won the Caldecott Medal in two consecutive years—in 1976 for *Why Mosquitoes Buzz in People's Ears* and in 1977 for *Ashanti to Zulu: African Traditions*. Read *Why Mosquitoes Buzz in People's Ears* and have students create a skit to retell the story. For their animal character, allow students to create a mask. Those students who do not have a speaking part can create a jungle mural that will act as background scenery.

4. Read *Ashanti to Zulu: African Traditions*. Have students create their own ABC book which retells traditions from the variety of groups that make up the United States. For example, the "P" page can tell about the Spanish piñata, while the "C" page could describe the chopsticks used by those who emigrated from Asia.

5. Encourage students to write a class letter to the Dillons (in care of their publisher), expressing their feelings about their illustrations, asking questions about their art and their method of working together, and so forth.

Chris Van Allsburg

This multi-talented artist, sculptor, author, and illustrator of children's books has had his work exhibited at numerous museums in the United States. He began his artistic career as a sculptor and went into painting quite by accident when another illustrator saw his drawings (which were initially done as a hobby) and encouraged him to illustrate books.

References

Helprin, M. (1989). *Swan Lake*. Illustrated by C. Van Allsburg. Boston: Houghton Mifflin.

Van Allsburg, C. (1982). *Ben's dream*. Boston: Houghton Mifflin.

† Van Allsburg, C. (1979). *The garden of Abdul Gasazi*. Boston: Houghton Mifflin.

* Van Allsburg, C. (1981). *Jumanji*. Boston: Houghton Mifflin.

Van Allsburg, C. (1990). *Just a dream*. Boston: Houghton Mifflin.

Van Allsburg, C. (1984). *The mysteries of Harris Burdick*. Boston: Houghton Mifflin.

* Van Allsburg, C. (1985). *The polar express*. Boston: Houghton Mifflin.

Van Allsburg, C. (1988). *The bad ants*. Boston: Houghton Mifflin.

Van Allsburg, C. (1983). *The stranger*. Boston: Houghton Mifflin.

Van Allsburg, C. (1983). *The wreck of the Zephyr*. Boston: Houghton Mifflin.

Van Allsburg, C. (1991). *The wretched stone*. Boston: Houghton Mifflin.

Van Allsburg, C. (1987). *The z was zapped: A play in twenty-six acts*. Boston: Houghton Mifflin.

Activities

1. Chris Van Allsburg's work has been exhibited in the Whitney Museum of American Art in New York City, the Museum of Modern Art in New York City, and The Grand Rapids Art Museum in Grand Rapids, Michigan, to name a few. Set up a classroom museum to display Van Allsburg's work. Have each student select a favorite book illustrated by Van Allsburg, and set up a display of the book along with objects that represent its pictures and content.

2. In *Ben's Dream*, the jacket illustration shows a picture of Mt. Rushmore, but with a humorous twist. Share this book with students and have them create a personalized version of Mt. Rushmore!

3. Random House has created many multi-media versions of Van Allsburg's books. This includes a cassette of *Jumanji, Ben's Dream,* and the *Wreck of the Zephyr.* They also have filmstrips with cassette of *The Polar Express* and *The Garden of Abdul Gasazi.* Try to obtain these versions to share with students.

4. One of Van Allsburg's signature elements is a small dog that is included in most of his books. Involve students in a search for this dog in the various Van Allsburg books they read.

5. In his Caldecott Award-winning book, *Jumanji,* Van Allsburg tells about two children who play a most unusual game. Read *Jumanji* to students and have them create their own board game modeled after the one in the story. Have them use their imaginations to create a picture that would go along with one of the boxes in the board game.

6. *The Polar Express,* which won Van Allsburg his second Caldecott Award, tells the story of a young boy who boards a mysterious train bound for the North Pole. Discuss with students the reason why so few people can hear the bell the little boy received from Mr. C. Have all the students imagine that each of them is on the Polar Express. Record an experience that each has on the Polar Express and have each student create an illustration to accompany his or her account of the experience.

Primary Unit: Counting and Computation

Theme: COUNTING AND COMPUTATION

Focus: Students will develop an intuitive feeling for numbers and their various uses and interpretations.

Objectives: On completion of this thematic unit, students will be able to:
1. Understand the numeration system and how it relates to counting.
2. Be able to do simple mathematical calculations.
3. Understand relative sizes of numbers.
4. Be able to use ordinal and cardinal numbers correctly.
5. Be familiar with small amounts of money.

Initiating Activity: Have the students brainstorm and then create a web of all the situations in which they use numbers. For example:

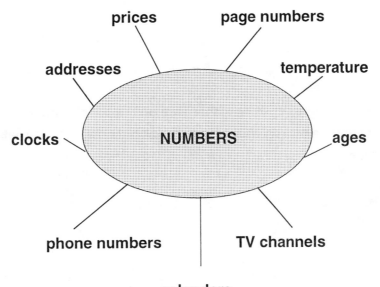

Discuss how their lives would be different if there were no numbers. If possible, share the book *The Day the Numbers Disappeared* by Leonard Simon and Jeanne Bendick.

General Activities:

1. Provide a selection of counting books for the children to peruse (the supplemental literature on p. 74–76 will provide some titles). Ask the children to work in cooperative learning groups to create their own counting books by using the books provided as models. Allow time to share books.

2. Ask the children to think of ways to keep track of things without using numbers. Allow time to share and discuss their ideas.

3. Ask the children to research how numerals are written in other cultures. Allow time to share different ways of writing the same numeral. *Number Act* by Leonard Fisher would be a helpful resource for this activity.

4. Ask the children to brainstorm songs, movies, sayings, phrases, and the like that use numbers—for example, "Tea for Two," "Walking on Cloud Nine," "Three Musketeers." Make a list of these and discuss what they mean.

5. Have the children help to create a math learning center that includes counting and other math-related children's books, assorted manipulatives, activity sheets, puzzles, etc. Prepare a "Math Solving Box" and then ask each child to write a story problem related to one of the children's books to put in the box. For example, if the book *One Watermelon Seed* by Celia Baker Lottridge was selected, the child could provide an ear of corn at the center and then submit the following problem:

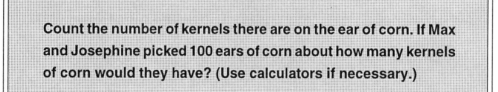

> **Count the number of kernels there are on the ear of corn. If Max and Josephine picked 100 ears of corn about how many kernels of corn would they have? (Use calculators if necessary.)**

Be sure each child puts the name of the book and his or her name on the problem submitted.

6. Make available a copy of *Anno's Math Games II* by Mitsumasa Anno. Assign the children to work in pairs as they select and figure out some of the puzzles, games, and activities. This could be an on-going activity over a period of a week or two. Allow time for each pair to select one of the puzzles, games, or activities to share, explain, or ask questions about.

7. Read the book *How Many Snails?* by Paul Giganti. Then assign different groups of children to investigate some of the questions presented in this book, or you and the children could generate your own "How many" questions. For example, how many clouds are in the sky, how many trees are in a nearby park or forest, how many birds are flying in the sky, etc.

Discussion Questions:

1. Who was born first in your family? second? third? (Answers may vary.)

2. What is the largest amount of money you have ever had? What did you do with it? (Answers may vary.)

3. How far can you count by one's, by two's, by five's, by ten's? (Answers may vary.)

4. Why is being able to count important? (Answers may vary.)

5. How would things be different if there were no numbers? (Answers may vary.)

Literature Related Activities

Title:	*The Doorbell Rang*
Genre:	Picture Book
Author:	Pat Huchins
Bibliographic Information:	William Morrow and Company, New York, 1989
Summary:	Ma bakes twelve cookies for Sam and Victoria (6 each). But just as they are about to eat the cookies, the doorbell rings and friends arrive. Each time a new set of friends arrive, Sam and Victoria divide up the cookies so everyone will have some. Finally, there are twelve children around the table with one cookie each and then the doorbell rings again. It is Grandma with a whole tray of cookies.
Interest Level:	Grades K–2.

1. Pre-Reading Activity:

    Show the children the illustration and read the text on the first page. Using one of your favorite simple cookie recipes, have the children help you measure the ingredients as you make a batch of cookies. Make the cookies as small as possible and then help the children divide the cookies among the group.

2. Learning Activities:

    a. Ask the children to estimate how many cookies were on Grandma's tray when she arrived. Then, ask them to pretend that they had to divide these cookies among the class. Help them to figure out how many cookies each child would get. Discuss the concept of division and that what is left over is the remainder. Ask the children to each write a brief paragraph and/ or illustrate what they would do with the remainder of the cookies.

    b. The children left their cookies on the table; however, the cat was sitting in the middle of the table. Ask the children to write story problems (on strips of paper) about the cat eating some of the cookies and how many would be left. (For example, there were 12 cookies on the table. The cat ate three cookies. How many cookies are left?) Put the story problems in a box and allow time for the children to select a problem, write it on the chalkboard, and provide an answer.

c. Ask the children to pretend that they are Victoria or Sam and that they can invite whomever they want to share the twelve cookies. Tell the children to make a list of who they would invite and to tell how many cookies each person would get.

d. Discuss party invitations and what information should be included in them. Then tell the children to create an invitation to send to the children they are inviting to their cookie party as described in Activity C. Allow time to share invitations.

e. Provide the children with kernels of corn, beans, or pieces of macaroni. Tell them to divide the pieces into piles of 12. Ask them to show how many different ways two children could divide 12 between them. Using the twelve cookies as an example, Victoria could have had eight cookies and Sam four, or Sam could have had 11 cookies and Victoria one. Tell them to lay out the different combinations of 12 pieces of corn, beans, or macaroni and then write the number problem it represents, that is, $8 + 4 = 12$, $11 + 1 = 12$.

3. Discussion Questions:

a. Do you think *The Doorbell Rang* is a good title for this book? Why or why not? (Answers may vary.)

b. How many children came to visit Victoria and Sam? (12) Why do you think they came? (Answers may vary.)

c. How do you think Victoria and Sam felt when children kept coming to the door and they had to share more and more of their cookies? (Answers may vary.)

d. What would have happened if there had been more children at the door instead of Grandma with the cookies? (Answers may vary.)

Title: *Numbers at Play: A Counting Book*

Genre: Informational

Author: Charles Sullivan

Bibliographic Information: Rizzoli International Publishing, Inc., New York, 1992

Summary: This book combines counting with poetry, art, and photography. It involves the children in counting objects in beautiful pictures by such artists as Gauguin and Renoir. Short biographies of each artist are also provided.

Interest Level: Grades K–4.

---

1. Pre-Reading Activity:

Obtain a photograph or painting that has a specific number of objects that can be counted, such as those provided in this book. Then ask the children to count the objects. Explain that this is the approach used by the author, Charles Sullivan, to illustrate the numbers one through ten. Then read the poems in the book and allow the children to count the objects in each picture.

2. Learning Activities:

a. As a class project, create a "Numbers at Play" by dividing the class into 10 groups. Assign each group a number (1 to 10) or, depending on grade level of the children, assign higher numbers. Tell each group to create an illustration that would include the number of objects that would represent their assigned number. Then, over a period of time, ask the entire class to assist in writing a poem to go along with the illustrations, as was done by Mr. Sullivan in *Numbers at Play*. When all the illustrations and poems have been completed, put them together in a booklet.

b. In the author's note at the end of the book, Mr. Sullivan, the author, said he likes to get letters from readers of his books telling him what they liked or disliked. As a group, write a letter to Mr. Sullivan telling him what you think about his *Numbers at Play* book, and also suggest some other photographs/paintings that he could use to illustrate the numbers 1 to 10 or higher.

c. Ask the children to look at each illustration to find other objects that could represent a number other than the objects pointed out by the author. For example, in William Henry Johnson's illustration entitled "Soapbox Racing," you could count the wheels (3) and make a poem about them, instead of counting the children (6).

d. Ask the children to look at pictures around the school, at home, in magazines, and so forth, and try to find objects in the pictures to count. A game could then be played by having the children bring in pictures to show the class and saying, "What do I see five of in this picture?" Allow time for the children to share their pictures and count objects.

3. Discussion Questions:

a. Which painting/photograph do you think best represents the number it is intended to represent? (Answers may vary.)

b. Do you like this kind of counting book? Why or why not? (Answers may vary.)

c. If you were writing a counting book, how would you do it? (Answers may vary.)

d. In which painting/photograph was it the most difficult to find the number of objects you were looking for? (Answers may vary.)

Title: *The Right Number of Elephants*

Genre: Picture Book

Author: Jeff Sheppard

Illustrator: Felicia Bond

Bibliographic Information: Scholastic, Inc., New York, 1992

Summary: This is a cleverly written book that counts backwards from 10 to 1 using elephants as the main characters.

Interest Level: Grades K–2.

1. Pre-Reading Activity:

    Ask the children the questions on the back of the book—How many elephants would you need to pull a train out of a tunnel and save everyone on board? to paint a ceiling? to escape a summer storm? Write their answers on the chalkboard and then compare them with what the book says.

2. Learning Activities:

    a. As a group, write a continuation of *The Right Number of Elephants* story using numerals 11 to 20. Assign groups to illustrate each of the numbers. Then compile the pages into a book for the class to read.

    b. Make available other counting backwards books, such as *Ten, Nine, Eight* by Molly Bang or *10 Bears in My Bed* by Stan Mack. Allow time for the children to compare and contrast the book(s) with *The Right Number of Elephants*.

    c. Make available the words to the song "The Twelve Days of Christmas." If possible, make one or more of the following books available as an aid: *The Twelve Days of Christmas* by June Williams; *The Twelve Days of Christmas* by Brian Wildsmith; *The Twelve Days of Christmas* by Jack Kent. Sing the song and then discuss the concept of counting backwards as a count down for a special event.

    d. As a follow-up to Activity C use the concept of counting down from a number (10 to 1) to count down for a special event such as a holiday, class party, or field trip. For example, if the class is having a party, you could plan the party by days. (For example, on the tenth day before the party we make invitations, on the ninth day we send invitations, on the eighth day we plan the food we will have, on the seventh day we decide who will bring what, and so on.)

3. Discussion Questions:

    a. Did you like this story? Why or why not? (Answers may vary.)

    b. Which of the tasks that the elephants did do you think could really happen? (Answers may vary.)

    c. Which of the tasks that the elephants did do you think couldn't really happen? (Answers may vary.)

    d. What is something some elephants might help you to do? How many elephants would you need? (Answers may vary.)

Title: *Anno's Counting Book*

Genre: Picture Book

Author: Mitsumasa Anno

Bibliographic Information: Thomas Y. Crowell, New York, 1986

Summary: This is a picture book without text that illustrates the numbers 0 to 12 through the growth of a community over months and years and through all seasons.

Interest Level: Preschool–Grade 2.

1. Pre-Reading Activity:

    Show the children the cover of the book and read the title. Ask them what they see that there is only one of (the moon), something there are two of (ladies), something there are three of (buildings), and so forth.

2. Learning Activities:

    a. Help the children to classify what they see on each page by asking them to identify one of the objects or people they see. For example, for number 1, write on the chalkboard as they name objects/people:

        1   moon

        1   tree

        1   snowman

        Continue through each page in the same manner.

    b. Help the children make clocks by using a paper plate, two black construction paper clock hands (one smaller than the other), and a brad in the center. Help them write the numerals around the outside of the plate. Starting with the page that represents the numeral 2, have the children look at the clock and then move the hands on their clocks to represent 2:00. Continue doing this on each page.

    c. Divide the children into groups and provide each group with a large sheet of paper. Assign each group a number and ask them to create a page of objects/people to represent the number they are assigned. Allow time for the children to share their pictures.

    d. Discuss the changes of seasons throughout the book—from 1 (January) to 12 (December). List the twelve months on the chalkboard, reread the book, and discuss the changes that take place each month.

3. Discussion Questions:

    a. Which counting page do you like best? Why? (Answers may vary.)

    b. Are there any pages where you couldn't find all the objects/people that were supposed to be there? If so, which ones? (Answers may vary.)

c. According to what the author wrote "About Numbers" on the last page of the book, how did people in the Stone Age keep records of what they did? (They drew pictures.)

d. Would you recommend this book to a friend? Why or why not? (Answers may vary.)

Culmination: The culminating activities will consist of a variety of activities that will involve using numbers. The children may do all or some of the following activities based on their level of ability.

1. Have the children spend an entire day without using numbers. For example, cover the clocks, remove watches, do not refer to page numbers for assignments, etc. Discuss how they felt the day went.

2. Play as many games as possible that require counting and/or using numbers—for example, "Mother, May I," where they have to take three steps forward, or six hops backward, etc.

3. Give directions using ordinal positions instead of names—for example, "Will the third person in the row open the door?"

4. Ask the children to write the largest number they can write and read correctly on a slip of paper, put their names on it, fold it and put it in a designated box. Pull each slip of paper from the box and call on the person who wrote the slip to read it. The child with the largest correct number can win a prize.

5. Ask the children to select a number to use as the focus of an illustration. For example, an 8 could become a snowman. Allow time to share.

Supplemental Literature

Primary (Grades 1–3):

Aker, S. (1990). *What comes in 2's, 3's, and 4's?* Illustrated by Bernie Karlin. New York: Scholastic.

A simple, delightful book that shows what comes in 2's—2 eyes, 2 ears. What comes in 3's—3 meals a day, 3 sizes—small, medium, large. What comes in 4's—wheels on a wagon, 4 legs on a table.

Allbright, V. (1985). *Ten go hopping.* London: Faber and Faber.

One little boy goes hopping and he is followed in turn by a grasshopper, a mouse, a frog, a rabbit, a cat, a dog, a monkey, a kangaroo, and an elephant.

Bang, M. (1983). *Ten, nine, eight.* New York: Greenwillow Books.

This is an enjoyable countdown-to-bed-time story that starts with "10 small toes all washed and warm" and ends with "1 big girl all ready for bed."

Falwell, C. (1993). *Feast for 10.* New York: Houghton Mifflin.

Numbers 1 to 10 are used to show how members of a family shop and work together to prepare a meal.

Fisher, L.E. (1982). *Number act.* New York: Four Winds Press.

    Portrays how numerals have looked in the past and how they look in other cultures.

Fleming, D. *Counting.* New York: Scholastic.

    A interestingly illustrated counting book from 1 to 10 that also includes counting by 10's to 50.

Giganti, P. (1988). *How many snails.* New York: Greenwillow Books.

    The author takes walks to various places, such as the lake, the beach, the garden, and so forth. Each time he gets to a different place, he wonders about the things he sees in each place and their different characteristics.

Keats, E.J. (1971). *Over in the meadow.* New York: Four Winds Press.

    A counting rhyme book that includes a host of mothers and their babies in their unique meadow habitats.

Lindberg, Reeve. (1987). New York: Dial Books.

    A story about a mother and son who tour a farm at midnight counting, in rhyme, the farm animals.

Lottridge, C.B. (1986). *One watermelon seed.* (1986). Toronto: Oxford University Press.

    Two children plant a garden with several seeds and plants. They water and weed and finally end up with many fruits and vegetables to pick. This book provides an opportunity for children to count from 1 to 10 as well as 10 to 100.

Mack, Stan. (1974). *10 bears in my bed.* New York: Pantheon Books.

    A little boy finds ten bears sleeping in his bed. He tells them to roll over and one by one they leave by the way of the window. Finally, all the bears are gone. This is an interesting countdown from 10 to 1 book.

Maestro, B. and Maestro, G. (1989). *Harriet goes to the circus.* New York: Crown.

    Harriet tries to be first in line to get into the circus. One-by-one her animal friends line up behind her. However, the entrance to the circus tent is at the other end of the line. Everyone turns around and now Harriet is last in line. This book provides a good introduction to ordinal numbers.

Princzes, E. (1993). *One hundred hungry ants.* Illustrated by Bonnie MacKain. Boston: Houghton Mifflin.

    One hundred hungry ants start out for a picnic but stop to change their line formation, which shows different divisions of 100. However, they lose both time and food in the end.

Trinca, R. and Argent, K. (1985). *One wooly wombat.* New York: Kane/Miller.

    Animals of Australia come forward and are counted in this beautifully illustrated counting book.

Intermediate (Grades 4–6):

Anno, M. (1982). *Anno's math games II.* New York: Philomel Books.

    Anno uses simple activities, picture puzzles, and games to introduce the mathematical concepts of multiplication, sequence, measurement, ordinal numbering, and direction.

Carlson, N. (1982). *Harriet's Halloween candy.* Minneapolis, MN: Carolrhoda Books.

    Harriet brings home a big bag of candy she got while trick-or-treating. When she gets home, she pours it out on the floor and sorts it according to size, color, and finally by her favorites. She then hides her candy in a variety of places until finally she eats it all.

Lieberthal, E.M. (1979). *The complete book of fingermath*. New York: McGraw-Hill.

Describes a simple technique for turning your ten fingers into a calculator.

Ockenda, S. and Doolittle, E. (1988). *World of wonders—A trip through numbers*. Boston: Houghton Mifflin.

A unique and interesting counting book that has detailed photographs for each number 1 to 12. The objects in the photographs depict a multitude of subjects that would interest a variety of people.

St. John, G. (1975). *How to count like a Martian*. New York: Henry Z. Walck.

This book provides an excellent introduction to other symbolic representation systems and base systems—Mayan, Greek, Chinese, Hindu, Egyptian, and Babylonian. The author explains how to count using an abacus and a computer.

Simon, L. and Bendick, J. (1963). *The day the numbers disappeared*. New York: Whittlesey.

This book, which is appropriate for grades K–6, allows the reader to sense the importance of the number system to our everyday lives.

Sitomer, M. and Sitomer, H. (1976). *How did numbers begin?* New York: Thomas Y. Crowell.

This book helps students think about the importance of numbers in our everyday lives and how the use of numbers evolved over the years.

Sitomer, M. and Sitomer, H. (1978). *Zero is not nothing*. New York: Thomas Y. Crowell.

Wyler, R. and Elting, M. (1992). *Math fun: Test your luck*. Illustrated by Patrick Girouard. New York: Simon & Schuster.

Presents interesting and enjoyable mathematical games, puzzles, tricks, and information about lotteries, number superstitions, lucky magic squares, etc.

MINI-THEMES

Addition and Subtraction

One of the first steps children need to take prior to actually doing the operations of adding and subtracting is learning the basic facts. By using the facts, plus an understanding of place value and mathematical properties, children will be able to successfully perform addition or substraction problems. Create an environment of stimulating and interesting math activities and related books such as those provided in this unit.

References

Brenner, B. (1989). *Annie's pet*. New York: Byron Preiss Visual Productions.

Burningham, J. (1980). *The shopping basket*. New York: Thomas Y. Crowell.

Chalmers, M. (1986). *Six dogs, twenty-three cats, forty-five mice and one hundred sixteen spiders*. New York: Harper & Row.

de Paola, T. (1989). *Too many hopkins*. New York: G.P. Putnam's & Son.

de Regniers, B.S. (1975). *So many cats*. New York: Clarion Books.

Dunbar, J. (1990). *Ten little mice*. Illustrated by Maria Majewska. San Diego: Harcourt Brace Jovanovich.

Giganti, P., Jr. (1992). *Each orange had 8 slices.* Illustrated by Donald Crews. New York: Greenwillow Books.

Gisler, D. (1991). *Addition Annie.* Chicago: Children's Press.

Mathews, L. (1980). *The great take-away.* New York: Dodd, Mead.

McMillan, B. (1986). *Counting wildflowers.* New York: Lothrop, Lee, and Shepard.

Schade, S. and Buller, J. (1991). *Hello! Hello!* New York: Simon & Schuster.

Walsh, E.S. (1991). *Mouse count.* New York: Harcourt Brace Jovanovich.

Whitney, D.C. (1966). *Let's find out about addition.* Illustrated by Harriet Sherman. New York: Watts.

Activities

1. Assign the children a number such as 10 and ask them to write out as many combinations as possible that add up to 10, for example, 4 + 6 = 10, 2 + 8 = 10, etc. Allow time to share their equations. Continue this process using other numbers.

2. Collect as many of the recommended books for this unit as possible. Ask the children to select one of the books, such as *Counting Wildflowers* by Bruce McMillan, *Each Orange Had 8 Slices* by Paul Giganti, Jr., or *The Great Take-Away* by Louise Mathews, and to create at least one addition or subtraction story problem that relates to the book. For example, a problem for *The Great Take-Away* might be the following: There were 10 ladies wearing necklaces at the masquerade party. After the robber pig left, only two ladies had necklaces. How many necklaces did the pig steal? Allow time to share books and problems.

3. As a group, write a story that involves giving away (subtracting) something (toys, pets, etc.). For example, it could be a story about a little old man who has 15 cats. He gives 2 cats to one neighbor. Now he has 13 cats. Next, his grandchild comes for a visit and she takes a cat. Now he has 12 cats. Continue the story until there are no cats. The book, *So Many Cats* by Beatrice Schenk de Regniers would be an interesting book to share before initiating this activity.

Large Numbers and Infinities

Large numbers—thousands, millions, billions, and trillions—are often difficult to comprehend because we do not usually experience them in everyday life. To give the children an insight into the enormity of a million, share David M. Schwartz's note "If You Wanted to Count..." at the end of his book *How Much Is a Million?* Schwartz explains that it would take 23 days, without stopping to eat or sleep, to count from one to one million. Children will enjoy experimenting with the activities provided in this mini-unit as they explore large and infinite numbers.

References

Ekker, E.A. (1985). *What is beyond the hill?* New York: J.B. Lippincott.

Gág, W. (1928). *Millions of cats.* New York: McCann.

Kalman, M. (1990). *Max makes a million.* New York: Viking.

McKissack, P. (1992). *A million fish . . . more or less.* New York: Alfred A. Knopf.

Modell, F. (1981). *One zillion Valentines.* New York: Greenwillow Books.

Schwartz, D.M. (1985). *How much is a million?* New York: Lothrop, Lee, and Shepard.

Activities

1. As a class project, begin collecting one million of something small, such as bottlecaps, buttons, small pebbles or seashells, etc. Display the collection in groups of tens or hundreds. Prior to initiating the collection, discuss and project how long it will take to collect the million items and how much space will be needed to display the collection. Record the projections. During the collection period, check accuracy of projection and revise, if necessary.

2. Divide the children into ten groups. Provide beans, corn, small macaroni, or some other small, inexpensive item for the children to count. Ask each group to count, in groups of ten, 100 of the items. Small paper muffin cups would work well for separating the items into groups of 10. When all groups have counted their set of 100, put all ten groups' 100's together to make a set of 1,000. Explain to the children that it would take a thousand sets of their set of 1,000 to make a million, a thousand sets of one million to make a billion, and a thousand billion to make a trillion. Write the following list on the chalkboard:

    Ten one hundreds = one thousand

    One thousand thousands = one million

    One thousand millions = one billion

    One thousand billions = one trillion

3. Make available as many of this unit's recommended books as possible. Allow time for the children to peruse the books. Then ask each child to share, with the class, something interesting they read about or an illustration in one of the books that relates to large numbers.

4. Tell the children to pretend that they have just won one million dollars and that they have to spend $1,000 per day. Remind them that it would take 1,000 days to spend their money because a million is one thousand thousands. Help them to calculate how many years, months, and days it would take to spend their money and what they could buy.

5. Tell the children to use the numerals 0 to 9 as many times as they want to make the largest and the smallest numbers they can make. Allow time for them to share their numbers as they write them on the chalkboard.

Money

Children often become involved with money prior to coming to school, although they do not recognize or understand the value of it. It is through a variety of experiences that children will learn to value money and use it correctly. Provide the children with as many real-life situations as possible in which money is used.

References

Froman, R. (1973). *Less than nothing is really something.* Illustrated by Don Madden. New York: Thomas Y. Crowell.

Hoban, L. (1981). *Arthur's funny money.* New York: Harper & Row.

Hoban, T. (1987). *26 letters and 99 cents.* New York: Scholastic.

Kimmel, E.A. (1989). *Four dollars and fifty cents.* New York: Holiday House.

Maestro, B. and Maestro, G. (1988). *Dollars and cents for Harriet.* New York: Crown.

McNamara, L. (1972). *Henry's pennies.* New York: Franklin Watts.

Schwartz, D.M. (1989). *If you made a million.* New York: Lothrop, Lee, & Shepard.

Viorst, J. (1978). *Alexander, who used to be rich last Sunday.* Illustrated by Ray Cruz. New York: Atheneum.

Activities

1. Many communities have a recycling program in which you get paid for recycling bottles, cans, newspapers, etc. As a group, investigate to find out what is available and then begin a class collection. Project how much money your class could make in a month and what you could buy with that amount.

2. Ask the children to identify something they would really like to have but do not have enough money to buy it. Next, tell them to find out exactly how much it would cost and to devise a plan for earning enough money to buy what they want. Finally, have the children implement their plan and keep a record of their progress. To initiate this activity, read *Dollars and Cents for Harriet* by Betsy and Giulio Maestro.

3. Provide children with some mail order catalogs or grocery ads from the newspapers. Divide the children into groups and tell them they have $50 to spend. Ask each group to make a list of things they would buy that will add up to no more than $50.

4. Set up a pretend restaurant or grocery store in which pretend money is used. Children can play different roles—waiter, waitress, customer, cashier, etc. A book such as Tana Hoban's *26 Letters and 99 Cents* could provide a useful resource for understanding different combinations of money.

Ordinal Numbers

Ordering or arranging things in a given sequence leads to ordinal numbers. The order may be related to such things as age (first-born, second-born), position in line (first, second), grades in school, etc. Children will enjoy the activities and books recommended for this mini-unit as they learn about ordinal numbers.

References

Bishop, C.H. (1938). *Five Chinese brothers.* New York: Coward-McCann.

Lasker, J. (1977). *Lentil soup.* Chicago: Albert Whitman.

Maestro, B. and Maestro, G. (1989). *Harriet goes to the circus.* New York: Crown.

Martin, B., Jr. (1970). *Monday, Monday, I like Monday*. New York: Holt, Rinehart, and Winston.

Mathews, L. (1982). *Cluck one*. New York: Dodd, Mead.

Activities

1. Ask the children to brainstorm situations where ordinals (first, second, third, etc.) are used. List them on the chalkboard—for example, games (who is first), position in a line, first paragraph or page, who wins first prize in a contest, etc. Then see if the children can identify a children's book that uses ordinals, for example, *Five Chinese Brothers* by Clare Hutchet Bishop.

2. Read a book, such as *The Year at Maple Hill Farm* by Alice and Martin Provensen, that presents the months of the year in an interesting manner. List the months on the chalkboard and choral read them. Discuss which is the first month, second month, etc. Provide the children with a worksheet on which the months are mixed up and ask them to write them in the correct order.

3. Help the children to learn about and utilize ordinal names of numbers by asking them questions such as what the character is doing on the *third* page of the book or who is sitting in the *second* seat in the *first* row. Next, ask each student to write one question using an ordinal name. Allow time for the children to ask and answer questions. *Harriet Goes to the Circus* by Betsy and Giulio Maestro is a good book to use to reinforce ordinal numbers.

4. Brainstorm with the children about all the "Firsts" that have happened throughout our history—for example, the first President of the United States, the first man/woman to walk in space, etc. Help the children to generate a list of "Firsts" in question form—for example, Who was the first President of the United States? Who was the first man to walk in space? Then allow time for them to find answers to all their questions.

INTERMEDIATE UNITS

Intermediate Unit: Saving Our Environment

Theme: SAVING OUR ENVIRONMENT

Focus: Students will develop an awareness of the beauty of the environment as well as an understanding of the critical environmental issues that require their attention.

Objectives: On completion of this thematic unit, students will be able to:

1. Grasp an understanding of the environmental problems facing our planet.

2. Learn some simple ways to help combat the problems facing our environment.

3. Learn about and understand the importance of saving our planet Earth.

4. Gain an understanding and appreciation for how the Earth's resources are a precious commodity that needs to be protected and nourished.

5. Learn more about the Earth's composition.

Initiating Activity: As a class, develop a survey about environmental issues related to saving the Earth. The directions for this survey should instruct the respondents to circle one of the following for each statement: Agree, Strongly Agree, No Opinion, Disagree, or Strongly Disagree. Students can be asked to use environmental books they have read to identify information they want to obtain from other people. Some sample statements the survey might include are these:

I believe it is important to separate garbage.

I believe people should continue to buy products made from the animals of the rain forest.

It is okay to burn or cut down part of a forest as long as we destroy it slowly.

I do not believe recycling is important.

I would be willing to support a project to save the environment.

I believe planting trees is important.

When the survey has been completed, ask the children to each interview at least ten people. Once the surveying has been completed, compile the results and make a graph to show the data.

General Activities:

1. Assist the children in learning to "interpret" the data from the initiating activity. Allow students to work in small groups to prepare a list of "findings" that can be reported to other classes as well as to their parents.

2. If the survey results in Activity 1 indicate that the people surveyed are in support of saving the Earth, then, as a class project, design a plan of action based on the most pressing environmental issues in your community. Then organize groups of people in your community to help you with various projects, for example, collecting newspapers, a campaign to collect money to plant trees, cleaning up a littered area, and so forth.

3. If the survey results in Activity 1 indicated lack of support for saving the Earth, organize an "Awareness Campaign" in which you inform your community of the importance of saving the environment. To do this, help your students develop a "fact sheet" about "Ways to Help Save Our Earth." Information for the fact sheet can be obtained from many sources, including books such as *50 Simple Things Kids Can Do to Save the Earth* by John Javna, or *Earth Book For Kids* by Linda Schwartz.

4. Ask the children to bring in an *old* white or light-colored T-shirt to class. Using fabric crayons (available in most craft stores) help the children design a T-shirt that sends an environmental message about saving the Earth.

5. Tell the children that today they are not going to be allowed to use any paper. They must do all their school work orally or on the chalkboard. At the end of the day, talk about how much paper the class saved. Brainstorm about other ways to save paper, which ultimately saves trees.

6. Many communities offer, and some even enforce, recycling campaigns that encourage trash sorting so that articles can be recycled easily. Make a graph on the chalkboard. Ask the children to fill in their names on the graph if their families sort and/or recycle any of the items that are listed.

EXAMPLE

Newspapers	Glass	Plastics	Aluminum Cans
Cheryl	Shari	Raquel	Denise
Saika	Shontevia		Cynthia
Shelly	Juan		Sadaka
			Samantha

7. Write "Help the Environment" in the middle of a circle drawn on the chalkboard. Have the students web things that need "help" in the environment. Have them work in groups to determine what is being done, in their homes or community, to "help" the environment, and to come up with additional ideas of what they can do to help solve the problem.

EXAMPLE   **Help the Environment**

air pollution   **rain forests**

water pollution   **endangered animals**

garbage

3. Write to one or more of the following environmentally friendly organizations requesting that they send you free information and/or a catalog of materials related to saving the Earth. Organize an area in the classroom to display the information you receive.

Alliance to Save Energy
1725 K Street, N.W., Suite 914
Washington, DC 20006

American Forestry Association
P.O. Box 2000
Washington, DC 20010

Global ReLeaf
The American Forestry Association
P.O. Box 2000
Washington, DC 20013

National Recycling Coalition
1101—30 Street, NW, Suite 305
Washington, DC 20007

U.S. Environmental Protection Agency (EPA)
401 M Street SW, A 108
Washington, DC 20460

Center for Action on Endangered Species
175 West Main Street
Ayer, MA 01432

Greenpeace   National Audubon Society
1611 Connecticut Avenue, NW   950 Third Avenue
Washington, DC 20009   New York, NY 10022

National Arbor Day Foundation   National Wildlife Federation
100 Arbor Avenue   1412—16 Street, NW
Nebraska City, NE 68410   Washington, DC 20036

9. Discuss the idea of forming an "Environmental Patrol Club" with your students. Discuss that this club would be made up of members who are interested in doing something to help save the environment. Members would actually "patrol" their neighborhoods looking for things that create problems for the environment. Once they have identified some problem areas, they should either take a picture of the problem, illustrate it, or write about it. Every day members will share what problems they observed and as a group problem solve what needs to be done to eliminate a particular problem. Then, individually or as a group, they take whatever steps are necessary to reverse the problem. This may require the assistance of other people or perhaps writing to your state representatives, senators, or one or more of the environmental agencies. Keep a log/scrapbook of what the club does to help save the environment. The club members may want to make club badges for the members to wear.

10. Ask the students to create bumper stickers that contain an environmental message. Remind them that bumper stickers need to be read quickly; therefore, the message has to be short and to the point. Display completed bumper stickers around the school and classroom.

Discussion Questions:

1. What do you perceive as the number one environmental problem confronting our planet today? What can be done to eliminate this problem?

2. Why doesn't everyone do their share to help save the Earth?

3. When did the planet Earth first begin to have problems with its environment? What has been happening over the years that has caused our many problems today?

4. What contributions are you (and your family) making to help save the environment?

Literature Related Activities

Title: *50 Simple Things Kids Can Do to Save the Earth*

Genre: Informational Book

Author: John Javna

Illustrator: Michele Montez

Bibliographic Information: Andrews & McMeel, Kansas City, MO, 1990

Summary: This book demonstrates how everyone's environment is connected to the whole world. It also provides information about how individuals can develop habits and projects that will help to save the environment. It is full of fun and exciting things to do that have environmental themes.

Interest Level: Grades 2 and up.

1. Pre-Reading Activity:

    Read the title, *50 Simple Things Kids Can Do to Save the Earth*. Then ask the students to each write one thing he or she can do to save the Earth. Share these orally, and then compile them onto one or two pages so that they can be duplicated and distributed. Be sure to include each student's name alongside his or her statement. You could title the collection "(number of students) Things (teacher's name) Class Can Do to Save the Earth." After reading the book, compare the students' list with the things presented in the book.

2. Learning Activities:

    a. On pages 11–17 of the book, information about acid rain, air pollution, disappearing animals, too much garbage, the greenhouse effect, the ozone layer, and water pollution is provided. Divide the class into seven groups and assign each group one of the topics. Allow them enough time to research and prepare a presentation on their assigned topic. The report could be, for example, a mural that depicts facts they have compiled, or it could be in the form of a skit, play, etc.

    b. On pages 18–19 of the book, there are quotes from children. Read these aloud. Keep the same assigned groups as in Activity "a." Ask the groups to write at least one quote about their topics. Allow time to share the quotes.

    c. Using the format used in this book for writing about each activity—"Take a Guess," "Did You Know," and "What You Can Do"—ask each student or small group of students to develop an environmental activity. Allow time to share the activities and compile them into a class booklet.

    d. Divide the class into groups and assign each group one of the "Eco-Experiments" on pp. 141–155 to plan and implement. Considerations regarding time of completion will need to be given based on availability of materials, length of experiment, and so forth. Allow time to share experiments and results.

3. Discussion Questions:

    a. What is the most important thing you learned about the environment from reading this book? How will what you learned help you and/or the environment?

    b. What changes have you made (regarding ways to save the environment) as a result of reading this book?

    c. What additional information would you have liked this book to have provided?

    d. If you could give this book to someone as a gift, who would you give it to? Why?

Title: *Earth Book For Kids*

Genre: Informational Book

Author: Linda Schwartz

Illustrator: Beverly Armstrong

Bibliographic Information: The Learning Works, Inc., Santa Barbara, CA, 1990

Summary: This book offers interesting and enjoyable environmental activities for children and
                    their families. It helps readers become better acquainted with their environment and
                    how to care for it.

Interest Level: Grades 2 and up.

1. Pre-Reading Activity:

    Read the title, *Earth Book For Kids.* Then ask the students to predict what the book is about, why
    anyone would want to write a book about the Earth, and if they have read any other books about
    the Earth. The students can record their predictions in individual environmental journals that
    can be added to as they proceed through this unit.

2. Learning Activities:

    a. As a group, write a letter to the author, Linda Schwartz, via the publisher's address in the
        front of the book. Tell the author such things as what you liked about the book and how it
        has or will help you to be more caring about the environment. Be creative about coming up
        with other things to communicate to her.

    b. There are two poems, written by children, on pages 183 and 184. Read these poems aloud.
        Then ask the students to write a poem that relates to preserving our environment.

    c. As a group, brainstorm and then make a list of things in your immediate environment that
        you think need attention. Then, using pages 132–137 as a guide, develop a plan of action and
        implement it. Ask several students to act as recorders during the project and to record the
        progress being made, changes you might make, goals you have achieved, etc.

    d. As a class project, create an environmental area in your classroom where displays of
        completed activities, collected materials, environmental trade books (see books listed in the
        Supplemental Literature bibliography), and so forth can be placed. Allow time and encour-
        age students to get involved in this area.

3. Discussion Questions:

    a. After reviewing the facts and information in this book, what do you think are the biggest
        environmental problems facing your community? your state? your country?

    b. What recommendations do you have for making this book better than it already is?

    c. Do you think your parents and people in your community are aware of all the problems
        facing the environment and what needs to be done? Explain.

    d. What do you think is the most important thing you can do to help save our planet Earth?

Title:	*Our Planet Earth*
Genre:	Informational Book
Author:	Lisa Feder-Feitel
Illustrator:	Peter Spacek
Bibliographic Information:	Scholastic, Inc., 1993
Summary:	Many facts about our planet Earth are provided, along with suggestions for taking care of it.
Interest Level:	Grades 2–5.

1. Pre-Reading Activity:

    Read the first page of the book (page 5) to the students. Then ask the students to write a brief story about what they think they would see if they were zooming around in space. Allow time to share these stories.

2. Learning Activities:

    a. Tell the students to become cartographers (map makers) by creating a map of the route from their homes to the school, or let them be creative and draw a map of their own choosing.

    b. Using the "Earth Facts" on page 32, plus other facts and vocabulary used in this book, help the students create a trivia card game. For example, one card could read, "The Earth is the _____ planet from the sun. (a) fourth, (b) third, (c) first, (d) last." Another card could read, "Scientists think there are _____ million other galaxies in the universe. (a) 5,000, (b) 25,000, (c) 10,000, (d) 1,000." Allow time to play the game.

    c. There are many different types of climate on our planet—some hot, some cold, some rainy, some dry. Ask the students to select the type of climate in which they would most like to live, find such a location, and then write a position paper on why they want to live there. Allow time to share.

    d. This book is brief and full of good information. Ask other teachers in your school if they would be willing to have some of the students from your class share this book with their class. Then assign a student or group of students to go into the class to read the book and then conduct a brief discussion about the book. The entire class may want to develop some discussion questions that would follow the reading of the book.

3. Discussion Questions:

    a. What is the most interesting fact you learned from reading this book? Why is this important?

    b. What makes up most of Earth's surface? (water) What are the four oceans? (Arctic, Atlantic, Pacific, and Indian)

    c. What is an archipelago? (a group of islands in an open sea) What are some examples of an archipelago? (Hawaii and the Philippines)

d. What are some of the things that are being done in an attempt to save our planet? What can you to do help?

Title: *Going Green: A Kid's Handbook to Saving the Planet*

Genre: Informational Book

Author: John Elkington, Julia Hailes, Douglas Hill, Joel Makower

Illustrator: Tony Ross

Bibliographic Information: Puffin Books, New York, 1990

Summary: *Going Green* provides a guide to saving the environment, including explanations of ecological issues and projects. Many facts about the environment and tips for getting involved in saving the environment are presented.

Interest Level: Grades 3 and up.

---

1. Pre-Reading Activity:

    Read the first page (page 5) of *Going Green*, "You Can Do It," aloud to the students. Record their answers to the last sentence: "So, what are you going to do?" Keep the list and refer to it several weeks later to check on what the students have done.

2. Learning Activities:

    a. The second part of the book is divided into "How Green Is Your Home?", "How Green Is Your School?" and "How Green Is Your Community?" Discuss what is meant by these questions. Divide the students into three groups. Assign each of the groups one of these questions and ask them to create a survey/audit that could be conducted that would answer the question. Allow time for them to implement the survey with the appropriate group of people. Compile data and share findings for each question.

    b. The authors of this book created an A to Z list of things that can be done to help save the planet (pp. 73–96). Help the students create their own A to Z list of ways to help save the environment, especially in their own communities. For example:

        A—<u>A</u>sk an environmentalist to speak with the class.

        B—<u>B</u>e careful and use less water.

        C—<u>C</u>all an environmental group in the yellow pages and ask how you can help.

        This could be made into an "Evironmental ABC Book."

    c. This book contains a list of facts about the greenhouse effect, the ozone layer, air pollution, acid rain, etc. Ask the students to work in groups to create fact-filled posters, flyers, etc. to distribute or post that would help inform the public about some of these problems.

    d. Ask students to select one environmental issue as a target project to become involved in. Then tell them to design a plan of action that would provide assistance with the project. For example:

Target Project: Using fewer paper bags.

Plan of Action: (1) Carry cloth or used bags.

                    (2) Refuse paper bags.

3. Discussion Questions:

   a. What do you see as the biggest problem facing the planet? Explain.

   b. What is the most interesting fact provided in this book?

   c. Has this book changed the way you feel about the environment? Why or why not?

   d. What one thing do you think you could do that would help save the environment? Explain why you think this would help.

Culmination: The culminating activity will be an "Earth Day." To do this, divide the students into groups. It is recommended that you divide the groups according to the four topics used for the mini themes—"Saving Our Forests," "Endangered Species," "Protecting and Preserving Our Waters," and "Trash and Garbage." Using these topics and/or others that the class decides on, ask each group to develop a center where they can gather information related to their topics, such as:

1. Trade books

2. Pamphlets, brochures, and other materials received from organizations

3. Demonstrations and experiments

4. Guest speakers and community people

5. Posters, bumper stickers

6. Handouts, for example, lists of ways to save water

7. Products developed during the environment unit

8. Costumes

9. A puppet show or skit

10. Displays, for example, a mock rainforest

Invite parents, community people, and other classes to visit the center. If possible, give each visitor a gift for coming, for example, a litter bag, a "Save the Environment" button or bumper sticker, a seedling for a tree, etc.

Supplemental Literature

Primary (Grades 1–3):

Baker, J. (1991). *Window*. New York: Greenwillow.

   This book, through wordless scenes observed from the window of his room, chronicles the events and changes in a young boy's life and his environment.

Cowcher, H. (1988). *Rain forests*. New York: Farrar, Straus and Giroux.

This beautifully illustrated book tells the simple story of the changes in the rain forest when it is threatened by man and machines. The animals manage to seek high ground and survive the initial phase of destruction but wonder how long they will be able to survive in the high trees of the forest.

Fernandez, K. (1991). *Zebo and the dirty planet.* Toronto, Canada: Annick Press.

Zebo lives on a planet where the air is clean and the water is clear. One day, when he looks through his telescope, he sees a dirty planet with animals that were looking sick. It made him sad and he decided to do something to help them.

Giles, J. (1989). *The first forest.* Stevens Point, Wis: Worzalla.

Through the element of nature, the reader is reminded that peace and harmony are good and that selfishness and greed are harmful. Show the children the cover of the book and read the title. Ask them to predict what the story will be about and to write their predictions on the board. After reading the story, review the predictions and compare them with what the story is actually about.

Glimmerveen, U. (1989). *A tale of Antarctica.* New York: Scholastic.

This is a moving story about Antarctica and how its landscape has changed because of pollution and litter. This well-illustrated book portrays, through the lives of charming penguins, the story of how the environment of Antarctica is threatened by man's presence.

Hirschi, R. (1992). *Where are my puffins, whales, and seals?* New York: Bantam.

This beautifully photographed book encourages children to understand that we cannot merely take from the sea and use it as a place to dump our waste, but we need to treat it with care to save the life that lives there. Children are introduced to the magnificent animals puffins, whales, and seals.

Jordan, M. and J. (1991). *Journey of the red-eye tree frog.* New York: Simon and Schuster.

Through the travels of a tree-frog, children learn about the many wonders of the rain forest. They are introduced to people, animals, and plants as well as the dangers to and within the rain forest.

Sheldon, D. (1990). *The whales' song.* New York: Scholastic.

This tells the story of a young girl, Lilly, whose grandmother loved the whales as a child and waited for them with a gift. The whales came to her with a special gift of their own. Now it's Lilly's turn to wait for the whales.

Stille, D.R. (1990). *Air pollution.* Chicago, IL: Children's Press.

This children's book, illustrated with color photos, describes air and its importance to humans. Air pollution and what we can do about it is also presented.

Tafuri, N. (1988). *Jungle walk.* New York: Greenwillow Books.

A young boy is reading a book about jungle animals as he falls asleep. Once asleep, he has a dream in which he meets all the animals. Ask the children what they think they would see if they went on a jungle walk.

Werenko, L.V. (1991). *It Zwibble and the greatest clean up ever!* New York: Scholastic.

The Zwibble family and their friends worked together to clean up a picnic area that was littered with trash and ruined by garbage.

Yolen, J. (1993). *Welcome to the greenhouse.* New York: Putnam's Sons.

The author presents a lush and poetic introduction to the rain forest. She points out that 50 acres of rain forest are being destroyed each minute and encourages readers to find out more about saving the rain forest.

Intermediate (Grades 4–6):

Hellman, Joan Rattner. (1985). *Tons of trash: Why you should recycle and what happens when you do.* New York: Random Publishing.

This book, printed on recycled paper, discusses what happens to recycled trash and what each person can do to dispose of trash in the environmentally best possible way.

Hoff, Mary and Rodgers, Mary M. (1992). *Our endangered planet: Life on land.* Minneapolis, MN: Lerner.

A look at endangered and extinct plants and animals is presented interestingly and clearly through well-chosen colored photographs and fascinating facts.

Johnson, Rebecca L. (1990). *The greenhouse effect: Life on a warmer planet.* Minneapolis, MN: Lerner.

Through photographs, charts, and diagrams, the greenhouse effect is explained, along with the possible impact it may have on our planet and its inhabitants.

Kalman, Bobbie. (1991). *Buried in garbage.* New York: Crabtree Publishing Co.

The reader will become aware of the reasons why garbage has become such a worldwide problem. They will also look at today's methods of disposing of garbage, what a landfill site is, and how incineration harms the environment.

Koral, April. (1989). *Our global greenhouse.* New York: Franklin Watts.

One book in a series that focuses on current ecological problems of the planet Earth.

Lampton, Christopher. (1992). *Coral reefs in danger.* Bookfield, CT: Millbrook Publishing.

This book explores the variety of causes—including pollution—that is contributing to the loss of the fragile ecosystem of coral reefs.

Lowery, Linda. (1991). *Earth day.* Pensacola, FL: Carolrhoda Books.

The ecological concerns and serious problems facing the world today are presented, along with activities and strategies to help do something about them.

Markle, Sandra. (1991). *The kids' Earth handbook.* New York: Atheneum.

Presents activities and experiments that demonstrate how living things interact with each other and the environment. Instructions are included for making miniature ecosystems.

McQueen, Kelly and Fassler, David. (1991). *Let's talk trash: The kid's book about recycling.* Burlington, VT: Waterfront Books.

This book presents the problems of solid waste disposal and highlights the idea that garbage is everybody's problem.

Miles, Betty. (1991). *Save the Earth.* New York: Knopf.

Save the Earth provides an overview of the environmental problems of land, atmosphere, water, energy, plants, animals, and people.

Pringle, Laurence. (1991). *Antarctica: Our last unspoiled continent.* New York: Simon and Schuster.

One of the country's foremost science writers presents an authoritative and interesting book about the continent Antarctica.

Sharpe, Susan. (1990). *Waterman's boy.* New York: Bradbury.

This excellent read-aloud book integrates an awareness of coastline ecology as it blends the plight of the Chesapeake Bay, the needs of the fishermen, and the needs of a young boy growing into manhood.

Viner, Michael and Hilton, Pat. (1991). *365 ways for you and your children to save the Earth one day at a time.* New York: Warner.

This book provides an activity/idea to help save the Earth for each day of the year.

Woodburn, J. (1992). *The acid rain hazard.* Milwaukee, WI: Gareth Stevens Publishing.

An informative book that discusses the causes of acid rain and how it affects the environment. It also provides information about ways to prevent and reverse acid rain and its effects.

Wurfbain, J. and L. (1990). *The education of Nagomo.* Huntington Beach, CA: Safari Press.

This story, written in the form of seven chapters, portrays the education of a young African boy called Nagomo about the plight of animals and the destruction of Africa. This children's book educates not just Nagomo, but everyone who listens to it. Particular attention is paid to the prevention of further destruction of the environment and the animals that live there.

MINI-THEMES

Saving Our Forests

Today there is great concern about conserving our forests, especially the rain forests. Over the past 100 to 150 years, much of the forest land has been cleared for farming and lumber. The destruction of these forests could be a disaster for the plants, animals, and people who live in the forests, as well as the environment in general. The following books and activities can help students become more aware of the dangers associated with destroying forests and provide some ways to help protect them.

References

Cherry, Lynne. (1990). *The great kapok tree.* San Diego, CA: Harcourt Brace Jovanovich.

Dorres, Arthur. (1990). *Rain forest secrets.* New York: Scholastic.

Lambert, David. (1990). *Forests.* Mahwah, NJ: Troll Associates.

Landau, Elaine. (1991). *Tropical rain forests around the world.* New York: Franklin Watts.

Luenn, Nancy. (1993). *Song for the ancient forest.* New York: Atheneum.

Rose, Deborah Lee. (1990). *The people who hugged the trees.* Niwot, CO: Roberts Rinehart, Inc.

Rosenblatt, Naomi. (1992). *Rainforests for beginners.* New York: Writers and Readers Pub., Inc.

Willow, Diane. (1991). *At home in the rain forest.* Watertown, MA: Charlesbridge Publications.

Activities

1. Trees for Life (1103 Jefferson, Wichita, KS 67203) is an organization that uses its profits to plant fruit trees in underdeveloped countries. For a fee of $.50 per student, the organization will send you seeds, individual cartons for planting, and a teacher workbook. The type of tree they send will depend on the state in which you live. They will send only trees that are native to your region. Students will enjoy watching their seeds sprout and finally grow into a tree.

2. As a class project, create a rain forest in your classroom. This can be done by making trees, vines, and animals out of old newspaper and throw-away items. One way to do this is to have each

student select an animal of the rain forest to research, report on, and make a replica of. Then the habitat for all these animals can be created cooperatively. Be sure to make available as many books as possible that relate to rain forests (see Supplemental Literature list). This would also be an excellent time to have a recycling center in your school or classroom, because it would emphasize the value of saving the rain forests.

3. Discuss the importance of recycling newspaper as a significant way of saving trees. Explain that approximately every four-foot stack of newspaper equals the wood from one tree. Designate one corner of the classroom or a hallway as a newspaper recycling center. Then ask the students in your class, as well as the entire school, to begin saving newspapers and stacking them in the designated area. Once a week, measure the stack of newspapers and record the measurement on a chart, placing a figure of a tree on the chart each time four feet of newspapers is collected. Take stacks of newspapers to local newspaper recycling centers when appropriate or arrange for them to be picked up.

4. As a group, brainstorm what you can do to help save the rain forests. For example:

   - Avoid buying products of the rain forests, such as things made of rosewood, teak, ebony, and mahogany.

   - Don't go to restaurants that use beef from cattle raised on land that used to be a rain forest. Ask where the beef comes from and explain why you are asking.

   - Write to your U.S. Senators and ask them to help protect rain forests.

     Mail letters to: Name of your Senator

     U.S. Senate

     Washington, D.C. 20515

   - Help inform others about the importance of saving the rain forest. Develop a plan of action for disseminating the brainstormed list of things to do to help save the environment that includes a time line. Revisit the list according to the time line established to see what has been accomplished.

5. Prior to initiating this activity, write to the National Arbor Day Foundation (100 Arbor Avenue, Nebraska City, NE 68410) and request a copy of "The Conservation Trees" brochure. This brochure describes how trees help the environment. Before sharing the brochure with the students, divide the students into cooperative learning groups and ask them to create their own brochure on how trees help the environment. Once the brochures are completed, display the students' brochures along with the one you received from the National Arbor Day Foundation. *Note:* If this is the students' first experience with making brochures, you will need to share some sample brochures with them.

6. Tell the students to try to count all the grocery bags that are being used by people leaving the grocery for 30 minutes, and then to realize that this is happening in all the groceries in their communities and around the world. Suggest that students carry and encourage others to carry cloth bags, paper or plastic bags saved from another trip, or a backpack the next time they go shopping. It is also recommended that the student explain to the clerks and others that the reason they are doing this is to help save a tree.

Endangered Species

Today, more than 100 names of animals appear on the list of endangered animals. This means that the population of these specific animals continually gets smaller and smaller until they risk becoming extinct, or completely disappearing from the environment. Animals become endangered for a variety of reasons: hunting and trapping, destruction of their habitats, poisoning, pollution, people collecting them, and so forth. The following books and activities can help students become more aware of which animals are endangered and what can be done to protect them.

References

Allen, Judy. (1992). *Tiger.* Cambridge, MA: Candlewick Press.

Darling, Kathy. (1991). *Manatee on location.* New York: Lothrop, Lee and Shepard.

Facklam, Margery. (1990). *And then there was one. The mysteries of extinction.* Sante Fe, NM: Sierra Club / Little, Brown.

Hirschi, Ron. (1992). *Where are my swans, whooping cranes and singing loons?* The National Audubon Society.

Pringle, Laurence. (1990). *Saving our wildlife.* Hillside, NJ: Enslow.

Sibbold, Jean H. (1990). *The manatee.* Minneapolis, MN: Dillon Press, Inc.

Stone, Lynne M. (1989). *Endangered animals.* Chicago, IL: Children's Press.

Woe, Jonathan. (1989). *The wing'ed whale from woefully.* Longboat Key, FL: Hawk Publications.

Wright, Alexander. (1992). *Will we miss them?* Waterton, MA: Charlesbridge.

Activities

1. As a class, write a letter to the Office of Endangered Species, Fish and Wildlife Services, U.S. Department of the Interior, Washington, D.C. 20240 and ask them to send you a copy of the list of endangered species. When you receive the list, check to see which, if any, of these species live in your area. Then come up with a plan of action for helping to protect the specie(s) living in your area. This plan may take the form of a campaign, posters, writing letters, etc. If none of the endangered species live in your area, select a species that lives in an area close to you to be the focus of this activity.

2. Where an animal lives is called its habitat. Humans call where they live a home or house. When humans want to find a place to live they look in the real estate ads. As a class, collect real estate ads and brochures to read. Display these on a bulletin board. Then ask the students to select an animal and to write a real estate ad that would attract that animal. Refer to the "humans' " real estate ads for ideas.

3. As a class, brainstorm to develop a list of ways to protect all animals and especially endangered animals. For example:

    Don't buy things made of furs and skins.

    Don't buy endangered animals as pets.

    Don't buy products that use some part of an endangered species, for example, elephant tusks.

Tell the students that once the list is developed, to use it to create a poster to display in your school or community.

4. Divide the students into pairs. Ask each pair to select one of the recommended books from this unit. Both students should read the book. Then ask one of the students to develop a telephone interview that might be held with one of the endangered species in the book. For example, the student might want to ask the species, How did you get to be an endangered species? How do you feel about being endangered? What can be done to help you? and so on. Once the phone interviews are developed, allow time for the students to interview their partner. Finally, as a whole group, discuss some of the questions and answers from the interview.

Protecting and Preserving Our Waters

All living things—plants, animals, and people—need water in order to survive. More than half of the people in America get their water from groundwater. We must be careful not to pollute groundwater by dumping toxic materials (gas, oil, paint, pesticides) onto the ground. Also, we must learn to conserve water, because each year more and more people are living on the planet Earth and they are using more and more of the water supply. Use the following books and activities to help the students learn more about protecting and preserving our Earth's water.

References

Cherry, Lynne. (1992). *A river ran wild*. San Diego, CA: Harcourt Brace Jovanovich.

Cole, Johanna. (1986). *The magic school bus at the waterworks*. New York: Scholastic.

Lewin, T. (1992). *When the rivers go home*. New York: Macmillan Publishing Co.

Spizman, R.F. and Garber, M.D. (1992). *Water*. Carthage, IL: Good Apple.

Stephen, R. (1990). *Rivers*. Mahivah, NJ: Troll Associates.

Activities

1. As a class, write to the following friendly environmental groups and ask them for materials related to protecting and preserving the waters of the Earth.

   Clean Water Action
   317 Pennsylvania Avenue, S.E.
   Washington, DC 20003

   Save Our Streams
   The Izaak Walton League of America
   1401 Wilson Blvd., Level B
   Arlington, VA 22209

   U.S. Environmental Protection Agency (EPA)
   410 M Street, S.W., A 108
   Washington, DC 20460

2. Discuss with the students that most people get their water from some type of city or town water system. These systems get their water from dammed-up rivers and streams or wells that get water from the underground. Some areas build aqueducts and lay pipe to carry water from other places. Most people who do not get their water from a city or town water system get their water out of wells, using underground water. Ask some local expert on your area's water system to

come in and explain where the water the students use comes from, what is done to ensure that the water is safe to drink, how adequate the supply is, and so on. This may also be a good time to explore ways to save water.

3. As a group, list all the ways in which the students use water—e.g., brushing teeth, drinking, cooking, flushing toilets, taking showers, doing laundry, washing cars, watering lawns and flowers, washing dishes, etc. Once the list has been completed, divide the students into groups. Assign each group two or three of the activities on the list to research to find out how much water is used. For example, it has been estimated that a five-minute shower uses approximately 25 gallons of water. After the research has been completed, list each of these activities and the amount of water used for each. Then, ask the students to individually calculate how much water they use in a week. Finally, discuss how they could cut down on their water use.

4. Ask the students to read at least one book that deals with protecting and preserving the Earth's water. Then tell them to critique it by giving special attention to (1) what was learned from reading the book, (2) how true and accurate was the information provided, (3) what should be done, if anything, as a follow-up to what was presented, (4) should the book be recommended to others—why or why not. Students should be encouraged to add additional information, if they want. Allow time to share.

5. Help the students set up the following experiment to find out how pure the water in their community is. Make available a small sieve or collander. Place a coffee filter in it. Then ask the students to collect small containers of water from a variety of sources—a nearby stream, lake, river, mud puddle, faucet, etc. Empty the water containers, one at a time, into the filter. Remove the filter, label the source of the water, and lay the filter in the sun to dry. Repeat with each sample of water. Observe to see which sample is the cleanest and which is the most polluted.

Trash and Garbage

People are making too much trash and garbage. We are running out of places to put them. It has been estimated that of the 6,000 landfills in the United States, by the year 2,000 half of them will be completely filled. Also, a lot of garbage ends up polluting streams and rivers, thus affecting animal life. Trash and garbage often becomes litter along our streets, highways, and in our parks. We need to begin to produce less garbage and to reuse and recycle the garbage we do produce. The following books and activities can provide the students with ideas and recommendations for dealing with garbage in a more productive manner.

References

Hadingham, Evan and Janet. (1990). *Garbage! Where it comes from, where it goes.* New York: Simon and Schuster.

Kalman, Bobbie. (1991). *Reducing, reusing, and recycling.* New York: Crabtree Pub. Co.

Pringle, Laurence. (1986). *Throwing things away: From middens to resource recovery.* New York: Crowell.

Savage, Candace. (1991). *Trash attack! Garbage and what we can do about it.* Buffalo, NY: Firefly Books Ltd.

Skidmore, Steve. (1991). *What a load of trash.* Illustrated by Thompson Yardley. Brookfield, CT: Millbrook Press.

Van Allsburg, Chris. (1990). *Just a dream.* Boston, MA: Houghton Mifflin Co.

Activities

1. Invite someone from the Department of Sanitation or other such appropriate department in your community to come to your class to discuss how the garbage in your community is handled. As a class, prepare questions for which you'd like to have answers. For example, How many tons of garbage is collected each week in your community? What happens to the garbage? Are people recycling? Is the amount of garbage produced increasing or decreasing? How long will we be able to dispose of garbage in the same manner as we are today? Finally, discuss what you as a class can do to help this process.

2. If possible, arrange a class visit to a recycling center in your community so that the students can better understand the proper way to sort garbage for recycling and also to learn the process of recycling. If you can't visit a recycling center, obtain as much information as possible about recycling from books and other sources, such as the National Recycling Coalition, 1101—30th Street, N.W., Suite 305, Washington, DC 20007. Then start a campaign for recycling in your community. This can be done by writing letters to the editor of the newspaper, and by making posters, flyers, bumper stickers, etc. Also, if every student in the class initiates and maintains a recycling program at his or her own home, that action alone will begin to make an impact on the community.

3. Ask the students to project how many pounds of garbage a day they think they produce and to write the prediction, along with their name, on a chart you have posted on the bulletin board, similar to the following:

Name	Predicted Pounds	Actual Pounds

Then ask them to carry a plastic garbage bag with them for 24 hours and to throw all their garbage into it. Remind them to include their portion of garbage produced at home during meal preparation, for example, empty cereal boxes, milk cartons, etc. At the end of the 24-hour period, tell the students to weigh their garbage and to record the weight on the chart. Then compare actual weights with predicted weight. Finally, do some calculations about what this amount of garbage means over a week, a year, a lifetime. Ask the question, How can we cut down on the garbage we produce?

4. As a class project or in small groups, adopt an area(s) in your community to keep litter free. This could be a park, your own school grounds, or along a stream or river. This may involve enlisting some cooperation from parents and community people. The students may even be able to collect money for aluminum and newspapers at recycling centers. They could save this money to beautify the area with trees and plants. As a class, make an impact!

Intermediate Unit: Multicultural Understanding

Theme: MULTICULTURAL UNDERSTANDING

Focus: Students will gain a sensitivity for the beliefs, values, and customs of other cultures through well-chosen literature and activities.

Objectives: On completion of this thematic unit, students will be able to:

1.   Identify the differences and similarities among cultures.

2.   Explain why people from other cultures immigrated to the United States.

3.   Recognize and gain insight into the prejudices and difficulties people of various cultures often face.

4.   Participate and appreciate games, celebrations, art, literature, and other activities/materials related to a variety of cultures and, therefore, better understand and value the cultural and literary diversity that is part of our society.

5.   Demonstrate a pride in their own heritage.

6.   Identify contributions made by other cultures to the United States.

Initiating Activity: Ask the students if they know how many people live on our Earth (approx. 5.5 billion). Then discuss with them in what ways these people are the same regardless of who they are or where they live, and in what ways they are different. Ask them if they feel it is necessary and/or important to learn about people who are different from themselves. Finally, read the book *People* by Peter Spier. After reading the book, discuss with the students what they were feeling and thinking as the book was being read.

General Activities:

1.   The Venn Diagram, developed by John Venn during the nineteenth century, was used in mathematics to compare two sets. Ask the students to use the Venn Diagram to compare themselves with one of the characters from the multicultural books they have read. To illustrate the Venn Diagram for the students, draw two overlapping circles on the chalkboard. Tell them to write adjectives that describe themselves in the circle labeled 1. In the circle labeled 2, write adjectives describing a character from the book. In the area labeled 3, list adjectives that describe both themselves and the character from the book.

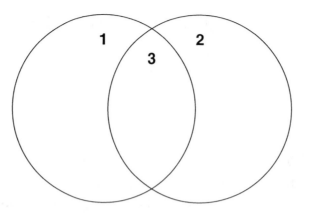

Note: The Venn Diagram can also be used to compare two religions, two particular holidays, two ethnic groups, and so forth.

2. Folk tales reflect the fundamental beliefs of a particular culture. Ask the students to read a folk tale from a country where one of their ancestors lived and to make a creative presentation to the class about the tale. The students may want to work cooperatively on their presentations (plays, skits, readers theatre, etc.). The presentations could be posters, dioramas, murals, etc. Encourage the use of such things as music, costumes, games, dances, and food that are appropriate to the culture in which the tale originated.

3. Help the students make a trivia card game about the characters, settings, themes, and so forth from the multicultural books they have been reading. For example, one trivia card might read— *The lotus seed was important to Ba because it reminded her of her country, _____ . (a) China, (b) United States, (c) Vietnam.* Encourage the students to each make at least one trivia card. Then allow time to play the game.

4. Although many people from other countries have settled throughout the entire United States, there are certain geographical areas that are more populated with people of a specific culture than other parts of the country are. For example, San Francisco and New York both have a large concentration of people from China. Divide the students into groups and assign each group people of a particular culture (Native Americans, African Americans, Hispanic Americans, Asian Pacific Americans, Jewish Americans). Then have the students do research to find out where the major concentration of their specific cultural group is and create a map of the United States that shows these concentrations of cultural groups. Display maps and allow time to discuss them. In the discussions, include the reasons why people of specific cultures tend to settle in one geographic area rather than another.

5. There are many conflicts still going on among and within various cultures. Ask the students to look through magazines and newspapers to find current articles about the problems that exist among the cultures being studied. Post these on a bulletin board and encourage all students to read them. Then involve the students in problem solving to solve a particular problem presented in one of the articles.

6. People from different cultures who have migrated to the United States have made many contributions in a variety of areas—music, art, science, economics, literature, and so forth. As a group, identify specific people who have made contributions and complete the following chart.

Name	Country of Origin	Contribution

Note: By posting the chart on a wall or bulletin board and adding new names as the occasion arises, this project can continue throughout the year.

7. In addition to the individuals identified in Activity 6, many **groups** of particular cultures who settled in America made enormous contributions to our development as a nation. For example, the Chinese are responsible for building much of the railway to the West, the first settlers for planting corn, and so on. Have each student select a contribution of one of the cultures being studied and illustrate it. Milton Meltzer's books, *The Black Americans: A History in Their Own Words, The Chinese Americans,* and *The Hispanic Americans,* can provide valuable insights into the various cultures. Display illustrations.

Discussion Questions:

1. Many people were forced to flee their countries, while others left their countries as a result of their own choice. Do you feel that the majority of the people who immigrated to America were glad they came here? Why or why not? (Answers may vary.)

2. If you decided you wanted to leave America and go to another country to live, where would you go? Why? What kind of things would be important to you to have in your "new country"? Who, if anybody, would you want to take along? (Answers may vary.)

3. Many people have to flee their countries without being able to take many of their personal belongings with them. What would be the most important thing(s) for you to take with you if you could only take what you could carry and manage readily? Explain. (Answers may vary.)

4. What reasons do people have for going to a new country to live? (Answers may vary.)

5. Do you think it is best for the people coming to America to become Americanized and to forget their own language, customs, and traditions? Or is it best for them to retain their own languages, customs, and traditions? Explain. (Answers may vary.)

Literature Related Activities

Title: *Class President*

Genre: Realistic Fiction

Author: Johanna Hurwitz

Bibliographic Information: Scholastic, Inc., New York, 1991

Summary: *Class President* is a story about how Julio developed leadership qualities as a result of an election of a fifth grade class president.

Interest Level: Grades 2–6.

1. Pre-Reading Activity:

    Discuss the fact that most organizations—from the government of the United States to a fifth grade class—all have presidents. As a group, brainstorm a list of qualities that a good president should have.

2. Learning Activities:

    a. Divide the class into pairs. Ask the students to create campaign slogans for their partners, for example, *"Vote for Liz, She's a Whiz."* Then use the slogan to make a poster that includes the partner's name and either a picture or a drawing of him or her. Allow time to share posters.

    b. It was mentioned in this story, *Class President*, that you have to be an American citizen to be elected President of the United States. Hold a class debate about the pros and cons of this rule.

    c. Divide the students into groups. Assign each group a country (for example, China, England, Japan, Spain), and ask them to research the process of electing a president or leader of the country assigned. Once the research has been completed, allow time to share the procedures used in other countries and to compare these procedures with those used to elect the President of the United States. Finally, evaluate which process of selecting a president or leader seems best.

    d. Julio was born in Puerto Rico. Discuss where the students in the class were born or the country in which their ancestors originated. Then attach a flat world map to the bulletin board/chalkboard and locate Puerto Rico on the map. Write Julio's name on a small white piece of paper 1" x 2", adhere it to the bulletin board/chalkboard and then attach a piece of yarn or string from Julio's name card to Puerto Rico. Continue this process with the students in the class and their families' ancestors.

3. Discussion Questions:

   a. Why do you think Julio had never mentioned that people didn't pronounce his name correctly? (Answers may vary.)

   b. Cricket brought up the point that you have to be an American citizen to be elected President of the United States and that Julio couldn't run for class president because he was born in Puerto Rico. How do you think Julio felt when she said that? Explain. (Answers may vary.)

   How do you think the other members of the class felt about this? Explain. (Answers may vary.)

   c. How is Julio's family similar to your family? How are they different? (Answers may vary.)

   d. Would you like to have Julio as a friend? Why or why not? (Answers may vary.)

Title: *The Lotus Seed*

Genre: Realistic Fiction

Author: Sherry Garland

Illustrator: Tatsuro Kiuchi

Bibliographic Information: Harcourt Brace Jovanovich, San Diego, 1993

Summary: A young Vietnamese girl's grandmother saw the emperor cry on the day he lost the throne. She took a lotus seed, which she carried with her everywhere, as a remembrance of her brave emperor and the homeland she had to flee.

Interest Level: Grades 2–4.

---

1. Pre-Reading Activity:

   Read the author's note aloud to the students and ask them to share what they know about Vietnam. Locate Vietnam on the map. Then ask the students to share what they think it would be like if suddenly they had to flee the United States because our government was overthrown.

2. Learning Activities:

   a. Invite someone who has lived in Vietnam (a refugee, if possible) to come to the class and discuss what Vietnam is like and provide information about the people who live there.

   b. There is a lot of controversy over the United States' role in the Vietnam War. Divide the class into two groups. Assign one group the role of supporting U.S. involvement in the war and the other group the role of not supporting U.S. involvement. Allow time for the students to research this topic and then have a debate.

   c. One day Bá and her family were crowded into a boat and sent to a strange land where they didn't even know the language. Ask the students to write a short story, in first person, describing this experience.

d. Assist the students in learning more about the Vietnamese culture by reading other books such as *First Snow* by Helen Coutant and Vo-Dinh; *Lee Ann: The Story of a Vietnamese-American Girl* by Tricia Brown; *Hoang Anh: A Vietnamese-American Boy* by Diane Hoyt-Goldsmith; *Hoang Breaks the Lucky Teapot* by Rosemary Breckler; and *The Land I Lost: Adventures of a Boy in Vietnam* by Quang Nhuong Huyug. After the students have had ample time to read some of the books, have a discussion period for them to share what they have learned from their readings.

3. Discussion Questions:

a. In this story, the parents chose the young man for their daughter to marry. What do you see as the pros and cons of this type of an arrangement? (Answers may vary.)

For students who are particularly interested in the concept of arranged marriages, you may want to recommend the book, *The Happiest Ending,* by Yoshido Uchida. This is a story about an attempt to prevent an arranged marriage between a young girl and an older man.

b. Do you think *The Lotus Seed* is a true story? Why or why not? (Answers may vary.)

c. Why was the lotus seed so important to the grandmother? (Answers may vary, but might include that it was the only remembrance she had of her homeland and the emperor.)

d. When Bá had to suddenly leave her home, the only thing she took was a lotus seed. If you were in a similar situation, what would you take? Why? (Answers may vary.)

Title:	*Tonweya and the Eagles and Other Lakota Indian Tales*
Genre:	Folktales
Author:	Rosebud Yellow Robe
Illustrator:	Jerry Pinkney
Bibliographic Information:	Dial Books for Young Readers, New York, 1979
Summary:	*Tonweya and the Eagles and Other Lakota Indian Tales* is a collection of nine stories told to Rosebud Yellow Robe by her father, Canowicakle. Canowicakle, known as Chano in these stories, lived with his people the Lakota-oyake, or Sioux nation, on the plains of what are now South Dakota, North Dakota, Nebraska, Wyoming, and Montana. In the foreword, we read about the real-life distinguished career of Canowicakle during the first quarter of this century. A glossary and pronunciation guide are also included.

Interest Level: Grades 3–5.

---

1. Pre-Reading Activity:

Read the title and tell the students that this is a collection of nine stories about Indians, told to the author by his father. Have the students discuss Indians they know about, such as Pocahontas and Sitting Bull. Ask students to discuss the good and bad qualities they see in these Indians and to predict how they think they will be different from and/or alike the Indians they are about to read about.

2. Learning Activities:

   a. Ask the students to work in cooperative groups as they select one of the stories from *Tonweya and the Eagles* and create a sequel for it. Allow time for the groups to share their stories.

   b. Read other Indian tales, myths, and legends, such as Olaf Baker's *Where the Buffalos Begin,* Paul Goble's *Girl Who Loved Wild Horses* or *Iktomi and the Berries.* Compare and contrast these stories with *Tonweya and the Eagles.*

   c. Brainstorm with the students how their lives differ from that of Canowicakle. Then, as a group or individually, have them make two lists, one about Canowicakle and one about themselves. How are the items on the lists alike? How are they different?

   d. In "The Lodge of the Bear," Chano saw a butte rising abruptly out of the plains. As he got closer, he noticed that it had long black lines running from top to bottom. His mother explained how the lines came to be. Tell the students that many folktales and myths offer explanations of why things are as we know them. Ask the students to create one of their own explanations. On the chalkboard, write out possible phenomena that could be explained in inventive ways. For example:

      Why do giraffes have long necks?

      Why do trees have leaves?

      Why does the sun rise in the east and set in the west?

      Have students select one and, in written form, explain it.

   e. Have the students prepare a list of Indian tribes on the chalkboard, such as Seminole, Cherokee, Sioux, Navajo, Cheyenne, and Apache. Divide the class into small groups and ask each group to select one of the Indian nations and research it. Provide class time so that each group can share what was learned.

   f. Discuss with the students how the stories in *Tonweya and the Eagles* were passed down through the family. Ask students to tell a story that has been passed down by someone in their families. If they do not know one, have them ask their parents and/or grandparents to share a story with them. They can start a storytelling tradition.

3. Discussion Questions:

   a. Which story did you like best? Explain. (Answers may vary.)

   b. Chano became known as a "bridge between two cultures." Why do you think he was described that way? (Answers may vary.)

   c. If you could have been with Chano through one event, which one would you pick? (Answers may vary.)

   d. Chano disobeyed his uncle and went on a buffalo hunt. Have you ever disobeyed anyone? If so, what happened? (Answers may vary.)

Title: *The Friendship*

Genre: Historical Fiction

Author: Mildred D. Taylor

Illustrator: Max Ginsburg

Bibliographic Information: Dial Books, New York, 1987

Summary: This story took place in 1933. Cassie and her three brothers were told by their parents that they could never go to the Wallace store. However, their Aunt Callie sent them to the store to get her some headache medicine. Once they got to the store, they were faced with the cruel prejudice of the store owners. Readers learn how white people and black people interacted during this period of time.

Interest Level: Grades 2–6.

1. Pre-Reading Activities:

    Ask the students to discuss what their neighborhoods might have been like 60 years ago. Then tell them that *The Friendship* story happened 60 years ago somewhere in the United States. Ask the students to predict how this story about friendship might be different if it occurred today in their town or city.

2. Learning Activities:

    a. Create a bulletin board about, *"Friendship."* Provide students with sheets of drawing paper that are folded in half. On the top half, ask each child to write a paragraph about the nicest thing a friend ever did for him or her. On the bottom half, ask them to illustrate the paragraph. Display the papers on the bulletin board.

    b. Compare how the situation in this story is similar to the situation in one of Mildred Taylor's other books, *Roll of Thunder, Hear My Cry.* Discuss whether situations like these still exist today and what should be done, if anything, to help improve relationships between different races of people.

    c. Have the students help you list all of the characters on the chalkboard.

Stacey	Dewberry Wallace
Christopher	John Thurston Wallace
Little Man	John Wallace
Cassie	Mr. Tom Bee
Jeremy Simms	Charlie Simms
	Aunt Callie Jackson

    Have students copy the list on a piece of paper. Beside each name have the students write down in phrase form how they feel about that character.

    Example: John Wallace—not trustworthy

d. Place the students in pairs. Ask them to discuss and decide, as a pair, their answers to these two questions:

  1. Will Mr. Tom Bee ever go back into the Wallace store again? Explain.

  2. When Mr. Tom Bee sees Mr. John Wallace, will he call him *John* or *Mr. John Wallace*? Explain.

  As a class, talk together about the answers each pair of students prepared. Is there general agreement about what might have happened?

3. Discussion Questions:

  a. What does Dewberry tell Little Man about his skin? (He tells him it is as black as dirt and if he put seeds on him they would grow in no time.) How does Little Man respond to this? (Answers may vary.)

  b. Why did John Wallace shoot Mr. Tom Bee in the leg as he left the store with his tobacco? (Answers may vary.)

  c. What did the children learn from this unforgettable day at the Wallace store? (Answers may vary.)

  d. Do you think that people still have the same ideas about names in today's world? Explain. (Answers may vary.)

  e. How would you define "friendship"? (Answers may vary.) What quality do you think is most important in a friend? (Answers may vary.) Have you ever been disappointed by a friend? Explain what happened. (Answers may vary.)

Culmination: The culminating activity will be making a class quilt that reflects the positive aspects of living within the diversity of many cultures. Students should be provided with a 12" x 12" piece of fabric or construction paper. They should then be asked to create an illustration, poem, pictures, or whatever medium they select that would best depict something that we, as a country, have gained as a result of all the immigrants who have come over the years. It may be something as simple as a drawing of an abacus with China written on it. Sew or glue the squares together to create a patchwork quilt that represents the cooperation among cultures and the gratitude America owes to all its immigrants. Be sure students write their names on their squares. Display the completed quilt.

Supplemental Literature

Primary (Grades 1–3):

Breckler, R.K. (1992). *Hoang breaks the lucky teapot*. Illustrated by Adrian Frankel. Boston, MA: Houghton Mifflin.

Vietnamese phrases and customs are brought out in this story of how Hoang diligently solves the problem created by breaking the teapot.

Brown, T. (1991). *Lee Ann: The story of a Vietnamese-American girl*. Illustrated by Thai. New York: Putnam.

This simple and informative story allows the reader to see Lee Ann doing many "American type activities," as well as enjoying special Vietnamese traditions such as the Tet celebration. Students will see the benefits of participating in two cultures.

Coutant, H. ànd Vo-Dink. (1974). *First snow*. New York: Knopf.

A sensitive story of a young Vietnamese-American girl who is dealing with the death of her grandmother as she experiences her first snowfall in New England.

Crews, D. (1991). *Bigmama's*. Fairfield, NJ: Greenwillow Books.

An autobiographical picture book about Donald Crews' childhood visits to his grandparents each summer.

Dorros, A. (1992). *Abuela*. Illustrated by Elisa Kleven. New York: Scholastic.

Portrays a loving relationship between a little girl and her *Abuela* (Spanish, meaning "grand-mother"). This book contains numerous Spanish words and phrases.

Gersten, M.J. (1992). *Why the sky is far away: A Nigerian folktale*. Illustrated by Carla Golembre. Waltham, MA: Joy Street (Little, Brown).

As a result of people being too greedy and taking more of the sky to eat than was needed, the sky moved far away so no one could reach it. Now the people have to grow and harvest their own crops.

Havil, J. (1992). *Treasure nap*. Illustrated by Elivia Savadier. Boston, MA: Houghton Mifflin.

A warm and tender story about how a mother tells her daughter the same nap-time story she was told as a child. The story is about how the little girl's Mexican great-grandmother said goodbye to her own grandfather as she immigrated to America with the treasures he had given her. When she awakens from her nap she carefully plays with the treasures.

Kurlin, S. (1992). *How my family lives in America*. Riverside, NJ: Bradbury Press.

This book introduces the reader to three young children—an African American, Hispanic American, and a Chinese American. These children describe their customs, families, and favorite foods and recipes.

McPherson, J. (1992). *Chasing games from around the world*. Austin, TX: Steck and Vaughn.

A book containing many easy-to-follow games from a wide variety of countries.

Ringgold, F. (1991). *Tar beach*. Westminster, MD: Crown.

A beautifully illustrated book that tells about a little girl who lives in an apartment in Harlem and how she flies over New York City.

Rodanas, K. (1991). *Dragonfly's tale*. Burlington, MA: Charion.

A Zuni Indian legend about how the Ashiwi tribe once harvested more corn than they could eat and the lessons they learned from the experience.

Say, A. (1992). *Grandfather's journey*. Boston, MA: Houghton Mifflin.

A poignant story of Allen Say's grandfather's immigration to the United States and return to Japan.

Strete, C.K. (1990). *Big Thunder Magic*. Illustrated by Craig Brown. Fairfield, NJ: Greenwillow Books.

A delightful story about the Great Chief and his trip to the city with his sheep Nanabee. A very small ghost, Thunderspirit, accompanies them and saves the day with his magic spirits.

Intermediate (Grades 4–6):

Hoyt-Goldsmith, D. (1992). *Hoang Ank: A Vietnamese-American boy*. Illustrated by Laurence Migdale. New York: Holiday.

A beautiful story about how a young boy, who was a baby when his parents fled Vietnam, is able both to be American and yet keep his Vietnamese traditions alive.

Huynh, Q.N. (1992). *The land I lost: Adventures of a boy in Vietnam*. New York: HarperCollins.

This book personalizes the Vietnamese people, which could help students become more positively acquainted with what has so often been represented as an alien land.

Kirkpatrick, H. (1990). *Toughboy and sister*. New York: McElderry/Macmillan.

Depicts a brother and sister who must draw on their Native American heritage to survive.

Soto, G. (1990). *Baseball in April and other stories*. San Diego: Harcourt Brace Jonvanovich.

Contains a collection of short stories depicting the daily lives of Hispanic children.

Spier, P. (1980). *People*. New York: Doubleday.

People investigates the similarities and differences among the four billion people on this Earth. It explores color of hair, eyes, and skin in addition to games, hobbies, feasts, holidays, religions, and so on.

Taylor, M.D. (1976). *Roll of thunder, hear my cry*. New York: Dial.

This book describes, with understanding, the black experiences of living in rural Mississippi during the 1930s. The story tells about the Logan family, which is determined not to let injustice go unchallenged.

Uchida, Y. (1985). *The happiest ending*. New York: Atheneum.

A story about an attempt to prevent the arranged marriage between a young girl and an older man. It provides an example of the struggles between the values of the Japanese Americans and the Japanese who came from Japan.

Uchida, Y. (1991). *The invisible thread*. Englewood Cliffs, NJ: Julian Messner.

This an autobiography of Yoshiko Uchida, in which she shares her experiences of growing up in Berkeley, California and in an American concentration camp as a second-generation Japanese American.

Wolfson, E. (1992). *The Teton Sioux: People of the plains*. Brookfield, CT: Millbrook Press.

Examines the history, culture, problems, and lifestyle of the Teton Sioux Indians.

Yep, L. (1975). *Child of the owl*. New York: Harper and Row.

Casey, a Chinese American girl, learns about herself as a Chinese American as a result of living with her grandmother in San Francisco's Chinatown.

Teacher References

McDonald, M.R. (1982). *The story teller's sourcebook: A subject, title and motif index to folklore collections for children*. New York: Gale Research Co.

Meltzer, M. (1984). *The black Americans: A history in their own words*. New York: Crowell.

Meltzer, M. (1980). *The Chinese Americans*. New York: Thomas Y. Crowell.

Meltzer, M. (1982). *The Hispanic Americans*. New York: Thomas Y. Crowell.

MINI-THEMES

Family Traditions

Among the various cultures, family traditions differ in terms of the food that is eaten, types and ways of celebrations, clothes that are worn, houses that are lived in, marriage ceremonies, and funeral rites. Although people from other cultures do become Americanized, many still retain some of their traditions. Students will enjoy discussing and experimenting with these traditions.

References

Garza, C.L. (1990). *Family pictures: Cuadros de Familia*. Chicago, IL: Children's Book Press. (Hispanic)

Hoyt-Goldsmith, D. (1991). *Pueblo storyteller*. Photos by L. Migdale. New York: Holiday House. (Native American)

Keegan, M. (1991). *Pueblo boy: Growing up in two worlds*. New York: Cobblehill/Dutton. (Native American)

Moore, E. (1988). *Whose side are you on?* New York: Farrar, Straus & Giroux. (African American)

Peters, R. (1992). *Clambake: A Wampanoag tradition*. Illustrated by John Madama. Minneapolis, MN: Lerner. (Native American)

Shalant, P. (1992). *Look what we've brought you from Mexico: Crafts, games, recipes, stories and other cultural activities from Mexican-Americans*. New York: Julian Messner/Simon and Schuster. (Hispanic)

Yee, P. (1991). *Roses sing on new snow: A delicious tale*. Illustrated by Harvey Chan. New York: Macmillan. (Chinese)

Activities

1. Ask the students to identify traditions, values, beliefs, and behaviors that are promoted in these books. Then compare and contrast these elements as they are demonstrated within and among the different cultures as well as within the students' own cultures.

2. *Pueblo Storyteller* and *Family Pictures* both offer a pictorial presentation of the lives of families from parallel cultures. Ask the students to create their own pictorial presentation of their families either through illustrations or photographs. Allow time for the students to share their creations and then to compare them with the two families represented in *Pueblo Storyteller* and *Family Pictures*.

3. Divide the students into groups, designate a group leader, and assign each group a book for which they will develop a Story Chart. For example, a Story Chart for *The Land I Lost: Adventures of a Boy in Vietnam* by Q.N. Huynh may look something like this:

Things Men Do farm hunt	**Things People Feared** wild boars tigers crocodiles
Things Women Do took care of home helped in fields	
Things People Ate rice eggplant meat Indian mustard	**Where People Live** hamlets along rivers and mountains houses made of bamboo
Things Girls Do weeded garden gathered eggs worked in kitchen	**Things Boys Do** some went to school herded buffalo fished

After all Story Charts have been completed, ask the group leader to report what ideas they included. You can then compare common headings such as *"Where People Live"* among the groups.

4. Ask each student to identify some object that represents a particular tradition in a culture, for example, piñata for Hispanics, totem pole for Native Americans, etc. Then ask them to provide a photograph, illustration, replica of the object or the real object, or whatever visual they select that will best demonstrate the object. Provide a table for displaying the objects and allow time to share and to explore them.

Language Patterns/Dialects

Sometimes, in order to retain the flavor of the language of the original storyteller, the writer of a folktale may use nonstandard language/dialect to tell the story. (It should be made very clear that all languages adequately serve their speakers and that no one language is better than another.) Readers of these folktales may find it difficult to adequately reproduce the dialect as written. Encourage the students to practice reading some of the following stories out loud.

References

Chase, R. (1943). *The Jack tales.* Illustrated by Berkeley Williams, Jr. New York: Houghton Mifflin.

Hamilton, V. (1983). *Willie Bea and the time the Martians landed.* New York: Greenwillow Books.

Lester, J. (1987). *The tales of Uncle Remus: The adventures of Brer Rabbit.* Illustrated by Jerry Pinkney. New York: Dial.

Smothers, E.F. (1992). *Down in the piney woods.* New York: Knopf.

Trosclair, P. (1973). *Cajun night before Christmas.* Gretna, LA: Pelican Pub. Co.

Yolen, J. (1990). *Sky dogs.* Illustrated by Barry Moss. San Diego: Harcourt Brace Jovanovich.

Activities

1. Discuss the variation in language styles and dialects in each book and the effects the variation produces for the reader.

    For example, select a sentence such as, *"Once the land winded us for we had to walk on our own legs from camp to camp…"* from Jane Yolen's *Sky Dogs.* Ask the students to discuss what is meant by this sentence and how they would write the sentence using standard English.

2. Pair students and ask them to select a book that contains nonstandard English/dialect. Then have them practice reading the language as written by reading to each other. A tape recorder can be helpful for this activity because it allows the readers to listen to themselves as well as to each other.

3. As a class, create a bibliography of books that are written in nonstandard English and/or contain dialects. This can be done by asking each student to submit at least one annotated bibliographical entry for such a book. If possible, display these books and allow time for the students to read each other's selection.

4. After the students have had sufficient time to read and experiment with nonstandard English/dialect writings, ask them to create a short story using nonstandard English/dialect. Allow time to share these stories.

Struggle for Freedom

From the beginning of time until the present time, people have struggled for their freedom. In fact, it was the English colonists' struggle for freedom that led to what is now America. This topic can be generalized by reading the recommended books and completing the activities, or by selecting a specific minority group or culture and elaborating on it.

References

Adler, D.A. (1989). *We remember the Holocaust.* New York: Henry Holt.

Cohen, B. (1983). *Molly's pilgrim.* Illustrated by Michael Deraney. New York: Lothrop, Lee and Shepard.

Ferris, J. (1988). *Go free or die: A story of Harriet Tubman.* Minneapolis: Carolrhoda.

Gordan, S. (1990). *The middle of somewhere.* New York: Orchard Books.

Hewett, J. (1990). *Hector lives in the U.S. now: The story of a Mexican American child.* New York: HarperCollins.

Kidd, D. (1991). *Onion tears.* Illustrated by Lucy Montgomery. New York: Orchard Books.

McKissack, P. and McKissack, F. (1989). *A long hard journey: The story of the Pullman Porter.* New York: Walker.

Miller, D. (1988). *Frederick Douglass and the fight for freedom.* New York: Facts on File.

Mohr, N. (1979). *Felita.* Illustrated by Ray Cruz. New York: Dial.

Activities

1. Tell the students to read one of the books recommended for this mini-unit or another book that deals with the struggle for freedom. After they have had time to read the books, ask the students to take on the role of the main character as they describe, to the class, the ordeal that he or she went through to achieve freedom.

2. Select one minority group or culture, for example, black slaves. As a class project, research and collect as much information as possible that depicts the struggle of this group for freedom. You may want to create a time line, mural, skit, TV show, or the like that would demonstrate their struggle. Invite another class or parents to attend the presentation of the findings of the group.

3. Today there are many groups struggling for freedom. As a class, identify these groups. Ask the class to bring in newspaper/magazine articles and post them on a bulletin board. After a few weeks, compare and contrast the struggle for freedom these groups are experiencing with the struggle of groups in the past.

4. Tell the students to imagine that they must suddenly leave where they live because they are no longer accepted and it is not safe to live there. Ask them to write a brief story describing what they would do. Allow time to share.

5. Invite someone who has gone through a struggle for freedom to come to class and ask them to share their experiences. Allow time for the students to ask questions.

Folklore

Every country has developed folktales or folklore that provides insight into its traditional wishes, dreams, humor, values, and other characteristics. Students who become acquainted with a variety of folk stories are well on their way to understanding what it means to live in a multicultural world.

References

Aardema, V. (1975). *Why mosquitoes buzz in people's ears.* Illustrated by Leo and Diane Dillon. New York: Dial. (African)

Dixon, A. (1992). *How raven brought light to people.* Illustrated by James Watts. New York: McElderry. (American Indian)

Fisher, L.E. (1986). *The Great Wall of China.* New York: Holiday House. (Chinese)

Galdone, P. (1974). *Little Red Riding Hood.* New York: McGraw-Hill. (American)

Geras, A. (1990). *My grandmother's stories: A collection of Jewish folktales.* New York: Knopf. (Jewish)

Hamilton, V. (1985). *The people could fly: American black folktales.* New York: Knopf. (African American)

Mahy, M. (Reteller). (1990). *The seven Chinese brothers.* Illustrated by J. and M. Tseng. New York: Scholastic. (Chinese)

Rohmer, H. and Wilson, D. (1987). *Mother scorpion country.* San Francisco: Children's Book Press. (Hispanic)

Roth, D. (1990). *The story of light.* New York: Morrow. (Native American)

San Souci, R. (1989). *The talking eggs: A folktale from the American South.* New York: Dial. (African American)

Yep. L. (1991). *Tongues of jade.* Illustrated by David Wiesner. New York: HarperCollins. (Chinese)

Young, E. (1989). *Lon Po Po: A Red Riding Hood story from China.* New York: Philomel. (Chinese)

Activities

1. Similar themes are found in folk tales from different countries. To introduce this concept to the students, compare two easy-to-read books, Ed Young's *Lon Po Po: A Red Riding Hood Story from China* and Paul Galdone's *Little Red Riding Hood,* by developing a Story Map like the following:

Comparing Two *Red Riding Hood* Tales	
Little Red Riding Hood (Galdone)	**Lon Po Po: A Red Riding Hood Story from China (Young)**
Country of Origin: United States	China
Characters: Wolf, Little Red Riding Hood, Woodsman, Grandmother	Shang, Tao, Paotze, Wolf
Setting: Woods and Grandmother's house	House and tree
Problem: The wolf ate the Grandmother and little Red Riding Hood.	The wolf wanted to eat the children.
Solution: A woodsman came by the house and cut the wolf open to free Red Riding Hood and her grandmother.	The children tricked the wolf into getting into the basket so he could reach the nuts and then they dropped him.
Consequence: They lived happily ever after.	The third time they dropped the wolf he died and the children returned to their house.

Following the discussion on the differences and similarities of these two tales, ask the students to select and compare two folktales using the Story Map format. For additional folktale information, refer to the book, *The Story Teller's Sourcebook: A Subject, Title, and Motif Index to Folklore Collections for Children* by Margaret Read McDonald, which provides an annotated bibliography of many folktales from other countries.

2. Discuss with the students that some folktales are "why" or "how" stories that are often referred to as *pourquoi stories*. Pourquoi stories explain the customs and characteristics of people as well as certain animal traits. Encourage the students to read books such as *Why Mosquitoes Buzz in People's Ears* by Verna Aardema or Susan Roth's *The Story of Light*. Ask the students to create their own pourquoi stories. Allow time to share.

3. Folktales of a particular culture reveal a lot about that culture. Assign groups of students a specific culture, such as African American, Native American, Hispanic, Asian American, and so forth. Tell them to collect as many folktales as possible for their assigned culture. Ask the students to read the folktales and to pay close attention to the illustrations as well as the animal characteristics or habits and natural phenomena. Allow each group to share the folktales and to report what they learned about their assigned culture. The students may want to chart what they learned from these tales using categories such as animals, foods, occupations, climate, homes, and so on.

4. Ask the students to select one folktale with which they will become very familiar. As a class project, arrange with kindergarten and first grade teachers for students to come into their classes to tell their folktales. Encourage the students to use necessary props and to practice their folktales prior to going into the classes. The school and/or local library may also be interested in having some folktales told to groups of children.

Intermediate Unit: Meet the Newberys

Theme: MEET THE NEWBERYS

Focus: Students will become involved with Newbery Award–winning literature and the authors whose works have inspired and excited the imaginations of readers.

Objectives: Upon completion of this thematic unit, students will be able to:

1. Become familiar with and read for enjoyment those books that have been awarded the Newbery Medal.

2. Become familiar with the authors of literature awarded the Newbery Medal.

3. Gain insight into the writing process and the ways ideas are generated and developed.

4. Identify and apply criteria for evaluating literature.

Initiating Activity: Discuss the significance of the Newbery Medal with students. The award is given to the author of the most distinguished contribution to literature published in the United States during the preceding year. (The author must be a citizen or resident of the U.S.) Have students suggest books they think should have been selected for the Newbery Award and list them on large chart paper. Then, go through the list of Newbery Award winners and honor books to see which of these have been recognized. At the completion of the unit, have students reassess their list and indicate whether or not they believe the same books should have been honored. Have them support their stand.

General Activities:

1. Involve students in reading various books that have been awarded the Newbery Medal. Have students identify the main subjects/topic each book focuses on and collaboratively create an annotated subject index for the Newbery Award winners. As students continue their reading, have them constantly update the index. If possible, include the books that were identified as Newbery Honor books as well. The index can then be used when planning thematic units.

2. Have students create a flag honoring a favorite Newbery Medal winner. Flags can be cut from various pieces of fabric and decorated with assorted materials to reflect something special about the book. Flags should also include the book's title and author. Encourage students to create individual flag holders so that flags can be displayed around the room.

3. Have students create a monthly newsletter that focuses on several Newbery Medal books each time. The newspaper can contain a variety of articles and features (comic strips, word searches, puzzles, advice columns, advertisements, and so on) related to the books being highlighted. Newsletters could be thematic—tied to the content being studied—and each month could be dedicated to books by a certain author, or based on books of a certain genre.

4. As a class, have students identify the criteria they think should be used to select the Newbery Medal for the most distinguished contribution to literature for children. On a large piece of butcher paper, create a chart with a column for titles and columns in which students can evaluate each book based on the criteria established. Assign each group of students a year between 1922,

when the Newberys were first awarded, and today. Have the students read the Newbery Medal winner and at least two honor books for their year. Have students evaluate the books based on the class criteria and place their evaluations on the class chart. Would they have selected the same book the American Library Association selected? Have students share their group's findings with the rest of the class, explaining the reasons for their evaluation.

Title	Criteria

5. Have students select a favorite author of a Newbery Medal winner. Have students research this author using such sources as *Something About the Author* (from Gale Publications—a reference found in most libraries). Have students, as a class, prepare an outline for reporting information he/she found most intriguing and then use this outline to create a biographical sketch of the author. Have students illustrate their report with illustrations representing one or more of the author's books. Compile these reports for a *Meet the Newbery Authors* reference book.

6. Have students create Tee Shirts that creatively represent their favorite Newbery Award–winning book. They can wear their shirts during the Culminating Activity.

7. Divide students into groups and have them each write three interpretive questions based on the book assigned after you have modeled several questions based on a book all of them are familiar with. (Interpretive questions are those for which there is no right or wrong answer. They can focus on a myriad of ideas, such as author purpose, character motivation, effect of the setting, and so on. Responses are based on individual interpretations but should be supported by specific references from the book.) Involve students in Literary Circles in which they each discuss one or more of the questions they developed with others in their group.

8. Each year the *Horn Book* publishes the acceptance speech of that year's Newbery Award–winning author. Involve students in reading the award-winning book and then read aloud the acceptance speech. Discuss the speech and the insights they gained.

9. Create a class poem honoring the Newbery winners. As a class, decide upon the rhyming pattern of the poem and write one verse together, based on one of the Newbery books all of them have read. Then, have students, in groups, create a verse for their assigned book, using the class verse

as a model. Have groups illustrate their verses and combine the work into a single poem. Send a copy to *Horn Book* or to magazines that publish student work.

10. Cereal companies are always looking for a new promotional idea to help them sell their cereals. Have students create a campaign that focuses on the heroes/heroines of children's literature. Have each student select a favorite Newbery Award–winning book character as the basis for the picture(s) and text for the front of a cereal box. Send copies of students' designs to one of the cereal companies, suggesting that the company do a series on children's literature.

Discussion Questions:

1. For whom was the Newbery Medal named? (John Newbery [1713–1767], the first English publisher of books for children.)

2. For what is the Newbery Medal awarded? (It is awarded to the most distinguished book of literature for children published in the United States during the preceding year.)

3. Do you believe awards such as the Newbery Medal are important? Why or why not?

4. Who is your favorite Newbery Medal author? Explain.

5. Which Newbery Medal award-winning book is your favorite? Explain.

6. What criteria do you believe are most important when evaluating books for the Newbery Award? Which criterion is the most important? Why?

Literature Related Activities

(*Note*: Each of the books in this section was awarded the Newbery Medal and each reflects a different literary genre.)

Title:	*The Witch of Blackbird Pond*
Genre:	Historical Fiction
Author:	Elizabeth George Speare
Illustrator:	—
Bibliographic Information:	Houghton Mifflin, Boston , 1958
Summary:	Kit Tyler journeys to Connecticut in 1687, and discovers a world quite different from her native Barbados. Her unconventional upbringing and her friendship with a Quaker woman isolates her from her Puritan neighbors and she is eventually brought to trial on the charge of witchcraft.
Interest Level:	Grades 5–8.

1. Pre-Reading Activity:

   Involve students in a clustering of the word, "Witchcraft." After the cluster has been completed, have each student select one word from the cluster and write a brief essay relating it to "witchcraft." Have students share their essays and discuss their perceptions of "witchcraft."

2. Learning Activities:

   a. Have students research life in New England in the late 1600s, and compare their findings with details from the book.

   b. As they are reading *The Witch of Blackbird Pond*, have students keep a simulated journal, one in which they write as if they are one of the main characters of the book. Allow time for students to share their journal entries and discuss their feelings/insights.

   c. Involve students in a mock trial in which they try Kit as a witch.

   d. Have students prepare and present persuasive speeches dealing with one of the issues reflected in *The Witch of Blackbird Pond*. For example, their speeches might focus on the issue of religious freedom, the issue of witchcraft, the issue of women's roles, etc.

   e. Elizabeth George Speare has been awarded the Newbery Medal for both *The Witch of Blackbird Pond* and *The Sign of the Beaver*. She is also the recipient of the prestigious Scott O'Dell Award for historical fiction for *The Sign of the Beaver*. Read additional books of historical fiction by Speare, such as *Calico Captive*, *The Bronze Bow*, and *The Sign of the Beaver*. Based upon the book read, group students and have them create a documentary to describe the life or time period presented in the book.

3. Discussion Questions:

   a. How would you describe Elizabeth George Speare's effectiveness as a writer of historical fiction? Explain.

   b. How would you describe life in late 17th-century New England?

   c. If you were to go back in time and live in the 1600s, what one thing would you miss most?

   d. Of all the characters in *The Witch of Blackbird Pond*, who do you admire least? Who do you admire most? Explain.

   e. Although we take pride in our modern-day technology, what things have changed little since the late 1600s?

Title:	*A Wrinkle in Time*
Genre:	Fantasy—Science Fiction
Author:	Madeleine L'Engle
Illustrator:	—
Bibliographic Information:	Dell, New York, 1962

Summary: Meg's father disappears and only she and her brother can save him. At the time of his disappearance, their father was working for the government on the concept of tesseract—a wrinkle in time. With the help of three unearthly strangers, Meg and Charles Wallace travel through time to a land of mystery and intrigue.

Interest Level: Grades 4–7.

1. Pre-Reading Activity:

   Discuss the title and its possible meaning. What do students believe a "wrinkle in time" might be?

2. Learning Activities:

   a. Have students create a large mural that illustrates all the wonders Meg and her brother discovered on their journey to save their father.

   b. *A Wrinkle in Time* is classified as Science Fiction by some experts because of its use of scientific terminology and facts. As students read the book, have them list the different scientific facts and select one to research. Have them share their findings by creating a game modeled after the television game show "Jeopardy."

   c. Have students imagine that their classrooms were controlled by "It." In groups, have them create a scenario and present it. After all the skits have been presented, have them discuss the dangers implicit when people give up their identities.

   d. As they search for their father, the children are aided by Mrs. Whatsit, Mrs. Who, and Mrs. Which. Have students select one of these women and create a clever "Wanted Poster" for her.

   e. Two other books by Madeleine L'Engle, *A Wind in the Door* and *A Swiftly Tilting Planet*, are companions to *A Wrinkle in Time*. Divide the class in half and have each group read one of the two books. Have each group give a creative Book Talk in which they try to interest the other group in reading the book.

   f. Use the opening line of the book, "It was a dark and stormy night," to create a class story—each student adds a paragraph. Encourage students to use detail and colorful characters. Tape the story as it is told and then transcribe it into book form for students to illustrate.

3. Discussion Questions:

   a. What is "tesseract." (A wrinkle in time.) Do you believe it is possible to travel by means of a wrinkle in time? Why or why not?

   b. Why is Meg better able to resist It? (She is able to confront It with the power of love, something It does not have or understand.)

   c. Of the three women—Mrs. Whatsit, Mrs. Who, and Mrs. Which, **who** is your favorite? **What** caused you to select her, and **which** scene involving this character did you enjoy most?

   d. How would you describe A *Wrinkle in Time* to someone who has never read it?

   e. What are the most important lessons of *A Wrinkle in Time?* (The importance of love and individuality.) Will these lessons be as important in the future? Why or why not?

Title: *Bridge to Terabithia*

Genre: Realistic Fiction

Author: Katherine Paterson

Illustrator: Donna Diamond

Bibliographic Information: Harper, New York, 1977

Summary: Two lonely people, Jess and Leslie, invent Terabithia, a magical kingdom they rule. When Leslie is killed in a freak accident, Jess must come to terms with her death and face the world with courage and the ability to imagine.

Interest Level: Grades 4–7.

1. Pre-Reading Activity:

    Explain to students that Terabithia is a magical kingdom in the woods, inspired by the imaginations of the book's two main characters, Jess and Leslie. Have each student describe what Terabithia might look like and compare it with what they discover from the book.

2. Learning Activities:

    a. Have students create their own Terabithia using any artistic media available.

    b. When Leslie was killed, Jess remembered all the wonderful things she had given him. Ask students to imagine that they are Jess and have them create either an epitaph (the inscription on a headstone that often tells something special about the person buried there) or a eulogy (a short speech given during a funeral that reminds everyone about the special qualities/contributions of the person who has died) for Leslie.

    c. Have students think about their goals for themselves and the things they hope to achieve in life. Have them create an epitaph for themselves. Encourage them to create epitaphs that are not only humorous but that, in some way, suggest their accomplishments.

    d. Have students, in groups, select a favorite scene from *Bridge to Terabithia* and present a dramatic interpretation of the scene.

    e. Many themes are suggested by *Bridge to Terabithia*—friendship, courage, growing up, and dealing with death. Have students select one of these themes and personify it, creating a verbal (essay) or visual (picture/sculpture) portrait of it—how it looks, tastes, feels, affects others, and so on.

3. Discussion Questions:

    a. What made Jess and Leslie's friendship so special?

    b. What did *Bridge to Terabithia* teach you about friendship?

    c. Is it important for children your age to have a special place like Terabithia? Describe your Terabithia.

d. *Bridge to Terabithia* was awarded the Newbery Medal. List five reasons why you think the book was so honored. Discuss your responses and try to reach a class consensus.

Title: *Lincoln: A Photobiography*

Genre: Biography

Author: Russell Freedman

Illustrator: Illustrated with Photographs and Prints

Bibliographic Information: Clarion, New York, 1987

Summary: The life and times of Abraham Lincoln as told through photographs, prints, and Russell Freedman's fascinating text.

Interest Level: Grades 4–7.

1. Pre-Reading Activity:

    What do students know about Abraham Lincoln? Ask students to individually list all the facts they know about Lincoln. Have them select the fact they believe is most interesting and create a picture to illustrate it. Have students use their illustrations to cover a large box—the Lincoln Artifact Box—which will be the focus of Learning Activity A.

2. Learning Activities:

    a. As students learn additional information about Lincoln, have each select a new fact or new impression about him they think is significant. Have the students create an object or locate some type of visual that represents this newly acquired fact or idea and place this in the artifact box created in the Pre-Reading Activity. At the conclusion of their study of *Lincoln: A Photobiography*, involve students in a discussion of the artifacts and the way in which each reflects Lincoln—his life and times.

    b. Have students create a *Photoautobiography* in which they tell about their own lives through pictures and text.

    c. Based on the insights they have gained about Lincoln, have groups of students create large collage caricatures of Lincoln that reflect Lincoln's personality and characteristics.

    d. It is often said that "a picture is worth a thousand words." Select a picture from the book that you believe especially supports this statement and write a brief essay that explains the photograph's impact. In small groups, have students discuss the pictures selected.

    e. Throughout the text, Freedman includes many of Lincoln's quotes. Have students select a favorite quotation, illustrate it (with original art or with pictures and cartoons), and combine their work into a book of sayings by Lincoln.

f.   At the back of the book is a list of other books about Lincoln. Have students read one more of these books and compare the insights and understandings about Lincoln that they gained from the book with those they gained from *Lincoln: A Photobiography.* Ask students: "Which book gave you the deepest understanding of Lincoln and his times?" "How was this accomplished?"

3.   Discussion Questions:

a.   How did the book reinforce or change your opinions and ideas about Abraham Lincoln?

b.   How did the photographs included in this book affect you?

c.   What did you learn about Abraham Lincoln that surprised you most?

d.   From your knowledge of Lincoln and his times, what do you think was the most difficult thing Abraham Lincoln had to face? Explain.

e.   Imagine that you are a children's literary critic. How would you rate *Lincoln: A Photobiography?* Explain your opinion.

Culminating Activity: "Meet the Newberys!" Involve students in a multi-media presentation of the best in children's literature. Each group of 3 to 4 students should select a favorite Newbery Award–winning book and present it to the audience in a creative way using one or more audio-visual materials and one or more dramatic forms (dance, music, art, storytelling, puppetry, etc.). Each presentation should be introduced by a creatively designed sign that includes the name of the book and its author, as well as names of the members of the group.

Invitations to this event should be sent to the school's faculty and classrooms, as well as to participants' parents. Decorate the room with book jackets, anthologies, newsletters, and the like that reflect the work done during this unit. You may have groups prepare food and drink that in some way represent the books being presented.

Supplemental Literature

The following is a list of those books that have been awarded the Newbery Medal or those that have been named Newbery Honor books.

1922   *The Story of Mankind* by Hendrik Willem van Loon, Liveright

Honor Books: *The Great Quest* by Charles Hawes, Little; *Cedric the Forester* by Bernard Marshall, Appleton; *The Old Tobacco Shop* by William Bowen, Macmillan; *The Golden Fleece and the Heroes Who Lived Before Achilles* by Padraic Colum, Macmillan; *Windy Hill* by Cornelia Meigs, Macmillan

1923   *The Voyages of Doctor Dolittle* by Hugh Lofting, Lippincott

Honor Books: No record

1924   *The Dark Frigate* by Charles Hawes, Atlantic/Little

Honor Books: No record

1925   *Tales from Silver Lands* by Charles Finger, Doubleday

Honor Books: *Nicholas* by Anne Carroll Moore, Putnam; *Dream Coach* by Anne Parrish, Macmillan

1926   *Shen of the Sea* by Arthur Bowie Chrisman, Dutton

Honor Book: *Voyagers* by Padraic Colum, Macmillan

1927   *Smoky, the Cowhorse* by Will James, Scribner's

Honor Books: No record

1928   *Gayneck, The Story of a Pigeon* by Dhan Gopal Mukerji, Dutton

Honor Books: *The Wonder Smith and His Son* by Ella Young, Longmans; *Downright Dencey* by Caroline Snedeker, Doubleday

1929   *The Trumpeter of Krakow* by Eric P. Kelly, Macmillan

Honor Books: *Pigtail of Ah Lee Ben Loo* by John Bennett, Longmans; *Millions of Cats* by Wanda Gág, Coward; *The Boy Who Was* by Grace Hallock, Dutton; *Clearing Weather* by Cornelia Meigs, Little; *Runaway Papoose* by Grace Moon, Doubleday; *Tod of the Fens* by Elinor Whitney, Macmillan

1930   *Hitty, Her First Hundred Years* by Rachel Field, Macmillan

Honor Books: *Daughter of the Seine* by Jeanette Eaton, Harper; *Pran of Albania* by Elizabeth Miller, Doubleday; *Jumping-Off Place* by Marian Hurd McNeely, Longmans; *Tangle-Coated Horse and Other Tales* by Ella Young, Longmans; *Vaino* by Julia Davis Adams, Dutton; *Little Blacknose* by Hildegarde Swift, Harcourt

1931   *The Cat Who Went to Heaven* by Elizabeth Coatsworth, Macmillan

Honor Books: *Floating Island* by Anne Parrish, Harper; *The Dark Star of Itza* by Alida Malkus, Harcourt; *Queer Person* by Ralph Hubbard, Doubleday; *Mountains Are Free* by Julia Davis Adams, Dutton; *Spice and the Devil's Cave* by Agnes Hewes, Knopf; *Meggy Macintosh* by Elizabeth Janet Gray, Doubleday; *Garram the Hunter* by Herbert Best, Doubleday; *Ood-Le-Uk the Wanderer* by Alice Lide and Margaret Johansen, Little

1932   *Waterless Mountain* by Laura Adams Armer, Longmans

Honor Books: *The Fairy Circus* by Dorothy P. Lathrop, Macmillan; *Calico Bush* by Rachel Field, Macmillan; *Boy of the South Seas* by Eunice Tietjens, Coward; *Out of the Flame* by Eloise Lownsbery, Longmans; *Jane's Island* by Marjorie Allee, Houghton; *Truce of the Wolf and Other Tales of Old Italy* by Mary Gould Davis, Harcourt

1933   *Young Fu of the Upper Yangtze* by Elizabeth Foreman Lewis, Winston

Honor Books: *Swift Rivers* by Cornelia Meigs, Little; *The Railroad to Freedom* by Hildegarde Swift, Harcourt; *Children of the Soil* by Nora Burglon, Doubleday

1934   *Invincible Louisa* by Cornelia Meigs, Little

Honor Books: *The Forgotten Daughter* by Caroline Snedeker, Doubleday; *Swords of Steel* by Elsie Singmaster, Houghton; *ABC Bunny* by Wanda Gág, Coward; *Winged Girl of Knossos* by Erik Berry, Appleton; *New Land* by Sarah Schmidt, McBride; *Big Tree of Bunlahy* by Padraic Colum, Macmillan; *Glory of the Seas* by Agnes Hewes, Knopf; *Apprentice of Florence* by Anne Kyle, Houghton

1935   *Dobry* by Monica Shannon, Viking

Honor Books: *Pageant of Chinese History* by Elizabeth Seeger, Longmans; *Davy Crockett* by Constance Rourke, Harcourt; *Day on Skates* by Hilda Van Stockum, Harper

1936   *Caddie Woodlawn* by Carol Brink, Macmillan

Honor Books: *Honk, The Moose* by Phil Stong, Dodd; *The Good Master* by Kate Seredy, Viking; *Young Walter Scott* by Elizabeth Janet Gray, Viking; *All Sail Set* by Armstrong Sperry, Winston

1937   *Roller Skates* by Ruth Sawyer, Viking

Honor Books: *Phebe Fairchild: Her Book* by Lois Lenski, Stokes; *Whistler's Van* by Idwal Jones, Viking; *Golden Basket* by Ludwig Bemelmans, Viking; *Winterbound* by Margery Bianco, Viking; *Audubon* by Constance Rourke, Harcourt; *The Codfish Musket* by Agnes Hewes, Doubleday

1938   *The White Stag* by Kate Seredy, Viking

Honor Books: *Pecos Bill* by James Cloyd Bowman, Little; *Bright Island* by Mabel Robinson, Random; *On the Banks of Plum Creek* by Laura Ingalls Wilder, Harper

1939   *Thimble Summer* by Elizabeth Enright, Rinehart

Honor Books: *Nino* by Valenti Angelo, Viking; *Mr. Popper's Penguins* by Richard and Florence Atwater, Little; *"Hello the Boat!"* by Phyllis Crawford, Holt; *Leader by Destiny: George Washington, Man and Patriot* by Jeanette Eaton, Harcourt; *Penn* by Elizabeth Janet Gray, Viking

1940   *Daniel Boone* by James Daugherty, Viking

Honor Books: *The Singing Tree* by Kate Seredy, Viking; *Runner of the Mountain Tops* by Mabel Robinson, Random; *By the Shores of Silver Lake* by Laura Ingalls Wilder, Harper; *Boy with a Pack* by Stephen W. Meader, Harcourt

1941   *Call It Courage* by Armstrong Sperry, Macmillan

Honor Books: *Blue Willow* by Doris Gates, Viking; *Young Mac of Fort Vancouver* by Mary Jane Carr, T. Crowell; *The Long Winter* by Laura Ingalls Wilder, Harper; *Nansen* by Anna Gertrude Hall, Viking

1942   *The Matchlock Gun* by Walter D. Edmonds, Dodd

Honor Books: *Little Town on the Prairie* by Laura Ingalls Wilder, Harper; *George Washington's World* by Genevieve Foster, Scribner's; *Indian Captive: The Story of Mary Jemison* by Lois Lenski, Lippincott; *Down Ryton Water* by Eva Roe Gaggin, Viking

1943   *Adam of the Road* by Elizabeth Janet Gray, Viking

Honor Books: *The Middle Moffat* by Eleanor Estes, Harcourt; *Have You Seen Tom Thumb?* by Mabel Leigh Hunt, Lippincott

1944   *Johnny Tremain* by Esther Forbes, Houghton

Honor Books: *These Happy Golden Years* by Laura Ingalls Wilder, Harper; *Fog Magic* by Julia Sauer, Viking; *Rufus M.* by Eleanor Estes, Harcourt; *Mountain Born* by Elizabeth Yates, Coward

1945   *Rabbit Hill* by Robert Lawson, Viking

Honor Books: *The Hundred Dresses* by Eleanor Estes, Harcourt; *The Silver Pencil* by Alice Dalgliesh, Scribner's; *Abraham Lincoln's World* by Genevieve Foster, Scribner's; *Lone Journey: The Life of Roger Williams* by Jeanette Eaton, Harcourt

1946   *Strawberry Girl* by Lois Lenski, Lippincott

Honor Books: *Justin Morgan Had a Horse* by Marguerite Henry, Rand; *The Moved-Outers* by Florence Crannell Means, Houghton; *Bhimsa, The Dancing Bear* by Christine Weston, Scribner's; *New Found World* by Katherine Shippen, Viking

1947 *Miss Hickory* by Carolyn Sherwin Bailey, Viking

Honor Books: *Wonderful Year* by Nancy Barnes, Messner; *Big Tree* by Mary and Conrad Buff, Viking; *The Heavenly Tenants* by William Maxwell, Harper; *The Avion My Uncle Flew* by Cyrus Fisher, Appleton; *The Hidden Treasure of Glaston* by Eleanore Jewett, Viking

1948 *The Twenty-one Balloons* by William Pène du Bois, Viking

Honor Books: *Pancakes-Paris* by Claire Huchet Bishop, Viking; *Li Lun, Lad of Courage* by Carolyn Treffinger, Abingdon; *The Quaint and Curious Quest of Johnny Longfoot* by Catherine Besterman, Bobbs; *The Cow-Tail Switch, and Other West African Stories* by Harold Courlander, Holt; *Misty of Chincoteague* by Marguerite Henry, Rand

1949 *King of the Wind* by Marguerite Henry, Rand

Honor Books: *Seabird* by Holling C. Holling, Houghton; *Daughter of the Mountains* by Louise Rankin, Viking; *My Father's Dragon* by Ruth S. Gannett, Random; *Story of the Negro* by Arna Bontemps, Knopf

1950 *The Door in the Wall* by Marguerite de Angeli, Doubleday

Honor Books: *Tree of Freedom* by Rebecca Caudill, Viking; *The Blue Cat of Castle Town* by Catherine Coblentz, Longmans; *Kildee House* by Rutherford Montgomery, Doubleday; *George Washington* by Genevieve Foster, Scribner's; *Song of the Pines* by Walter and Marion Havighurst, Winston

1951 *Amos Fortune, Free Man* by Elizabeth Yates, Aladdin

Honor Books: *Better Known as Johnny Appleseed* by Mabel Leigh Hunt, Lippincott; *Gandhi, Fighter Without a Sword* by Jeanette Eaton, Morrow; *Abraham Lincoln, Friend of the People* by Clara Ingram Judson, Follett; *The Story of Appleby Capple* by Anne Parrish, Harper

1952 *Ginger Pye* by Eleanor Estes, Harcourt

Honor Books: *Americans Before Columbus* by Elizabeth Baity, Viking; *Minn of the Mississippi* by Holling C. Holling, Houghton; *The Defender* by Nicholas Kalashnikoff, Scribner's; *The Light at Tern Rock* by Julia Sauer, Viking; *The Apple and the Arrow* by Mary and Conrad Buff, Houghton

1953 *Secret of the Andes* by Ann Nolan Clark, Viking

Honor Books: *Charlotte's Web* by E. B. White, Harper; *Moccasin Trail* by Eloise McGraw, Coward; *Red Sails to Capri* by Ann Weil, Viking; *The Bears on Hemlock Mountain* by Alice Dalgliesh, Scribner's; *Birthdays of Freedom*, Vol. 1 by Genevieve Foster, Scribner's

1954 *. . . and now Miguel* by Joseph Krumgold, T. Crowell

Honor Books: *All Alone* by Claire Huchet Bishop, Viking; *Shadrach* by Meindert DeJong, Harper; *Hurry Home Candy* by Meindert DeJong, Harper; *Theodore Roosevelt, Fighting Patriot* by Clara Ingram Judson, Follett; *Magic Maze* by Mary and Conrad Buff, Houghton

1955 *The Wheel on the School* by Meindert DeJong, Harper

Honor Books: *The Courage of Sarah Noble* by Alice Dalgliesh, Scribner's; *Banner in the Sky* by James Ullman, Lippincott

1956 *Carry on, Mr. Dowditch* by Jean Lee Latham, Houghton

Honor Books: *The Secret River* by Marjorie Kinan Rawlings, Scribner's; *The Golden Name Day* by Jennie Lindquist, Harper; *Men, Microscopes, and Living Things* by Katherine Shippen, Viking

1957 *Miracles on Maple Hill* by Virginia Sorensen, Harcourt

Honor Books: *Old Yeller* by Fred Gipson, Harper; *The House of Sixty Fathers* by Meindert DeJong, Harper; *Mr. Justice Holmes* by Clara Ingram Judson, Follett; *The Corn Grows Ripe* by Dorothy Rhoads, Viking; *Black Fox of Lorne* by Marguerite de Angeli, Doubleday

1958   *Rifles for Watie* by Harold Keith, T. Crowell

Honor Books: *The Horsecatcher* by Mari Sandoz, Westminster; *Gone-Away Lake* by Elizabeth Enright, Harcourt; *The Great Wheel* by Robert Lawson, Viking; *Tom Paine, Freedom's Apostle* by Leo Gurko, T. Crowell

1959   *The Witch of Blackbird Pond* by Elizabeth George Speare, Houghton

Honor Books: *The Family Under the Bridge* by Natalie S. Carlson, Harper; *Along Came a Dog* by Meindert DeJong, Harper; *Chucaro: Wild Pony of the Pampa* by Francis Kalnay, Harcourt; *The Perilous Road* by William O. Steele, Harcourt

1960   *Onion John* by Joseph Krumgold, T. Crowell

Honor Books: *My Side of the Mountain* by Jean George, Dutton; *America Is Born* by Gerald W. Johnson, Morrow; *The Gammage Cup* by Carol Kendall, Harcourt

1961   *Island of the Blue Dolphins* by Scott O'Dell, Houghton

Honor Books: *America Moves Forward* by Gerald W. Johnson, Morrow; *Old Ramon* by Jack Schaefer, Houghton; *The Cricket in Times Square* by George Selden, Farrar

1962   *The Bronze Bow* by Elizabeth George Speare, Houghton

Honor Books: *Frontier Living* by Edwin Tunis, World; *The Golden Goblet* by Eloise McGraw, Coward; *Belling the Tiger* by Mary Stolz, Harper

1963   *A Wrinkle in Time* by Madeleine L'Engle, Farrar

Honor Books: *Thistle and Thyme* by Sorche Nic Leodhas, Holt; *Men of Athens* by Olivia Coolidge, Houghton

1964   *It's Like This, Cat* by Emily Cheney Neville, Harper

Honor Books: *Rascal* by Sterling North, Dutton; *The Loner* by Esther Wier, McKay

1965   *Shadow of a Bull* by Maia Wojciechowska, Atheneum

Honor Book: *Across Five Aprils* by Irene Hunt, Follett

1966   *I, Juan de Pareja* by Elizabeth Borten de Trevino, Farrar

Honor Books: *The Black Cauldron* by Lloyd Alexander, Holt; *The Animal Family* by Randall Jarrell, Pantheon; *The Noonday Friends* by Mary Stolz, Harper

1967   *Up a Road Slowly* by Irene Hunt, Follett

Honor Books: *The King's Fifth* by Scott O'Dell, Houghton; *Zlateh the Goat and Other Stories* by Isaac Bashevis Singer, Harper; *The Jazz Man* by Mary H. Weik, Atheneum

1968   *From the Mixed-Up Files of Mrs. Basil E. Frankweiler* by E. L. Konigsburg, Atheneum

Honor Books: *The Black Pearl* by Scott O'Dell, Houghton Mifflin; *The Egypt Game* by Zilpha Keatley Snyder, Atheneum; *The Fearsome Inn* by Isaac Bashevis Singer, Scribner; *Jennifer, Hecate, Macbeth, William McKinley, and Me, Elizabeth* by E. L. Konigsburg, Atheneum

1969   *The High King* by Lloyd Alexander, Holt, Rinehart & Winston

Honor Books: *To Be a Slave* by Julius Lester, Dial; *When Shlemiel Went to Warsaw and Other Stories* by Isaac Bashevis Singer, Farrar, Straus & Giroux

1970 *Sounder* by William Armstrong, Harper & Row

Honor Books: *Journey Outside* by Mary Q. Steele, Viking; *Our Eddie* by Sulamith Ish-Kishor, Pantheon; *The Many Ways of Seeing: An Introduction to the Pleasures of Art* by Janet Gaylord Moore, Harcourt Brace Jovanovich

1971 *The Summer of the Swans* by Betsy Byars, Viking

Honor Books: *Enchantress from the Stars* by Sylvia Louise Engdahl, Atheneum; *Kneeknock Rose* by Natalie Babbitt, Farrar, Straus & Giroux; *Sing Down the Moon* by Scott O'Dell, Houghton Mifflin

1972 *Mrs. Frisby and the Rats of Nimh* by Robert C. O'Brien, Atheneum

Honor Books: *Annie and the Old One* by Miska Miles, Atlantic-Little; *The Headless Cupid* by Zilpha Keatley Snyder, Atheneum; *Incident at Hawk's Hill* by Allan W. Eckert, Little, Brown; *The Planet of Junior Brown* by Virginia Hamilton, Macmillan; *The Tombs of Atuan* by Ursula K. LeGuin, Atheneum

1973 *Julie of the Wolves* by Jean C. George, Harper & Row

Honor Books: *Frog and Toad Together* by Arnold Lobel, Harper & Row; *The Upstairs Room* by Johanna Reiss, Crowell; *The Witches of Worm* by Zilpha Keatley Snyder, Atheneum

1974 *The Slave Dancer* by Paula Fox, Bradbury

Honor Book: *The Dark Is Rising* by Susan Cooper, Atheneum

1975 *M. C. Higgins, the Great* by Virginia Hamilton, Macmillan

Honor Books: *Figgs and Phantoms* by Ellen Raskin, E. P. Dutton; *My Brother Sam Is Dead* by James Lincoln Collier and Christopher Collier, Four Winds; *The Perilous Gard* by Elizabeth Marie Pope, Houghton Mifflin; *Philip Hall Likes Me, I Reckon Maybe* by Bette Greene, Dial

1976 *The Grey King* by Susan Cooper, Atheneum

Honor Books: *Dragonwings* by Laurence Yep, Harper & Row; *The Hundred-Penny Box* by Sharon Bell Mathis, Viking

1977 *Roll of Thunder, Hear My Cry* by Mildred Taylor, Dial

Honor Books: *Abel's Island* by William Steig, Farrar, Straus & Giroux; *A String in the Harp* by Nancy Bond, Atheneum

1978 *Bridge to Terabithia* by Katherine Paterson, Crowell

Honor Books: *Anpao: An American Indian Odyssey* by Jamake Highwater, Lippincott; *Ramona and Her Father* by Beverly Cleary, Morrow

1979 *The Westing Game* by Ellen Raskin, Dutton

Honor Book: *The Great Gilly Hopkins* by Katherine Paterson, Crowell

1980 A *Gathering of Days: A New England Girl's Journal, 1830–32* by Joan W. Blos, Scribner

Honor Book: *The Road from Home: The Story of an Armenian Girl* by David Kerdian, Greenwillow

1981 *Jacob Have I Loved* by Katherine Paterson, Crowell

Honor Books: *The Fledgling* by Jane Langton, Harper & Row; *A Ring of Endless Light* by Madeleine L'Engle, Farrar, Straus & Giroux

1982 *A Visit to William Blake's Inn: Poems for Innocent and Experienced Travelers* by Nancy Willard, Harcourt Brace Jovanovich

Honor Books: *Ramona Quimby, Age 8* by Beverly Cleary, Morrow; *Upon the Head of the Goat: A Childhood in Hungary, 1939–1944* by Aranka Siegal, Farrar, Straus & Giroux

1983   *Dicey's Song* by Cynthia Voigt, Atheneum

Honor Books: *The Blue Sword* by Robin McKinley, Greenwillow; *Doctor DeSoto* by William Steig, Farrar, Straus & Giroux; *Graven Images* by Paul Fleischman, Harper & Row; *Homesick: My Own Story* by Jean Fritz, Putnam; *Sweet Whispers, Brother Rush* by Virginia Hamilton, Philomel

1984   *Dear Mr. Henshaw* by Beverly Cleary, Morrow

Honor Books: *The Sign of the Beaver* by Elizabeth George Speare, Houghton Mifflin; *A Solitary Blue* by Cynthia Voigt, Atheneum; *Sugaring Time* by Kathryn Lasky, Macmillan; *The Wish Giver* by Bill Brittain, Harper & Row

1985   *The Hero and the Crown* by Robin McKinley, Greenwillow

Honor Books: *Like Jake and Me* by Mavis Jukes, Alfred A. Knopf; *The Moves Make the Man* by Bruce Brooks, Harper & Row; *One-Eyed Cat* by Paula Fox, Bradbury

1986   *Sarah, Plain and Tall* by Patricia MacLachlan, Harper & Row

Honor Books: *Commodore Perry in the Land of the Shogun* by Rhoda Blumberg, Lothrop, Lee & Shepard; *Dogsong* by Gary Paulsen, Bradbury

1987   *The Whipping Boy* by Sid Fleischman, Greenwillow

Honor Books: *A Fine White Dust* by Cynthia Rylant, Bradbury; *On My Honor* by Marion Dane Bauer, Clarion; *Volcano: The Eruption and Healing of Mount St. Helen's* by Patricia Lauber, Bradbury

1988   *Lincoln: A Photobiography* by Russell Freedman, Clarion

Honor Books: *After the Rain* by Norma Fox Mazer, Morrow; *Hatchet* by Gary Paulsen, Bradbury

1989   *Joyful Noise: Poems for Two Voices* by Paul Fleischman, Harper & Row

Honor Books: *In the Beginning: Creation Stories from Around the World* by Virginia Hamilton, Harcourt Brace Jovanovich; *Scorpions* by Walter Dean Myers, Harper & Row

1990   *Number the Stars* by Lois Lowry, Houghton Mifflin

Honor Books: *Afternoon of the Elves* by Janet Taylor Lifle, Watts; *Shabanu: Daughter of the Wind* by Suzanne Fisher Staples, Knopf; *The Winter Room* by Gary Paulsen, Watts

1991   *Maniac Magee* by Jerry Spinelli, Little, Brown

Honor Book: *The True Confession of Charlotte Doyle* by Avi, Jackson/Orchard

1992   *Shiloh* by Phyllis Reynolds Naylor, Atheneum

Honor Books: *Nothing But the Truth: A Documentation Novel* by Avi, Jackson/Orchard; *The Wright Brothers: How They Invented the Airplane* by Russell Freedman, Holiday House

1993   *Missing May* by Cynthia Rylant, Jackson/Orchard

Honor Books: *The Dark-thirty* by Patricia McKissack, Knopf; *Somewhere in the Darkness* by Walter Dean Myers, Scholastic; *What Hearts?* by Bruce Brooks, HarperCollins

1994   *The Giver,* by Lois Lowry, Houghton Mifflin

Honor Books: *Crazy Lady!* by Jane Leslie, HarperCollins; *Eleanor Roosevelt: A Life of Discovery,* by Russell Freedman, Clarion; *Dragon's Gate,* by Laurence Yep, HarperCollins

1995   *Walk Two Moons,* by Sharon Creech, HarperCollins

Honor Books: *Catherine, Called Birdy,* by Karen Cushman, Clarion; *The Ear, the Eye and the Arm,* by Nancy Farmer, Jackson/Orchard

MINI-THEMES

Introducing the Classics

While contemporary children's literature is popular with children today, rarely are they introduced to the classics. It is important that children also be exposed to those books that have withstood the test of time and are still considered outstanding examples of children's literature.

References

(For purposes of this mini-theme, books identified as classics are those originally published before the second half of the twentieth century. The original publishing date is listed after the publisher.)

Alcott, L. M. (1968). *Little women*. Illustrated by J. W. Smith. Boston, Little. (1868)

Barrie, J. M. (1980). *Peter Pan in Kensington Gardens*. Illustrated by A. Rackham. Buccaneer Books. (1906)

Baum, Frank. (1980). *The Wizard of Oz*. Illustrated by M. Hague. New York: Holt. (1900)

Brink, C.R. (1970). *Caddie Woodlawn*. New York: Macmillan. (1935)

Burnett, F. H. (1981). *Little Lord Fauntleroy*. Buccaneer. (1886)

Burnett., F. H. (1989). *The secret garden*. Illustrated by S. Hughes. New York: Viking. (1910)

Carroll, L. (1988). *Alice's adventures in Wonderland*. Illustrated by A. Browne. New York: Knopf. (1865)

Collodi, C. (1988). *The adventures of Pinocchio*. Illustrated by R. Innocenti. New York: Knopf. (1891)

Cooper, J. F. (1986). *The Last of the Mohicans*. Illustrated by N.C. Wyeth. New York: Scribner's. (1826)

Dodge, M. M. (1988). *Hans Brinker, Or the silver skates*. New York: Scholastic. (1865)

DuBois, W. P. (1947). *The twenty-one balloons*. New York: Viking.

Estes, E. (1974). *The hundred dresses*. San Diego: HBJ. (1944)

Forbes, E. (1943). *Johnny Tremain*. Illustrated by L. Ward. Boston: Houghton.

Grahame, K. (1983). *The wind in the willows*. Illustrated by J. Burningham. New York: Viking. (1908)

Kipling, R. (1950). *The jungle books*. Illustrated by F. Eichenberg. New York: Grosset. (1894)

Kipling, R. (1991). *Just so stories*. Illustrated by D. Frampton. New York: HarperCollins. (1902)

Lawson, R. (1944). *Rabbit Hill*. New York: Viking.

Milne, A. A. (1988). *Winnie the Pooh*. Illustrated by E.H. Shepard. New York: Dutton. (1926)

Scott, W. (1964). *Ivanhoe*. Airmont. (1820)

Sewell, A. (1945). *Black Beauty*. New York: Grosset. (1877)

Spyri, J. (1982). *Heidi*. Illustrated by T. Howell. New York: Messner. (1884)

Stevenson, R. L. (1985). *A child's garden of verses*. Illustrated by M. Foreman. New York: Delacorte. (1885)

Stevenson, R. L. (1981). *Treasure Island*. Illustrated by N.C. Wyeth. New York: Scribner's. (1883)

Travers, P. (1934). *Mary Poppins*. San Diego: HBJ.

Twain, M. (1989). *The adventures of Tom Sawyer*. Illustrated by B. Moser. New York: Morrow. (1876)

Verne, J. (1988). *Around the world in eighty days*. Illustrated by B. Moser. New York: Morrow. (1872)

Verne, J. (1986). *Journey to the center of the earth*. New York: Penguin. (1864)

Verne, J. (1964). *Twenty thousand leagues under the sea*. Airmont. (1869)

Wiggin, K. D. (1986). *Rebecca of Sunnybrook Farm*. New York: Penguin. (1903)

Wyss, D. (1981). *The Swiss Family Robinson*. Sharon. (1814)

Activities

1. Involve students in a "Meeting of Minds" in which students take on the persona of a favorite author of a favorite classic and become members of a panel in which they discuss their writing.

2. After reading a favorite classic, have groups create a time capsule that includes objects, photographs, and the like that represent the book and its time. Have students share their time capsule with other classes to encourage students to read the classics.

3. After reading a classic, involve students in a discussion of the way in which the development of theme compares with the way in which a similar theme is dealt with today. Have students create a Venn Diagram to depict their findings.

Theme: The Family

Little Women   *Ramona and Her Father*

by Louisa May Alcott (1868)   by Beverly Cleary (1977)

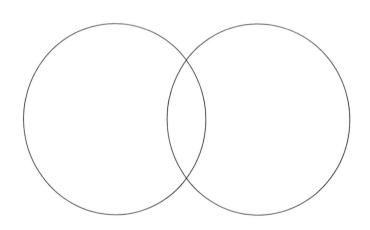

4. After reading one of the classics, have students select one of the main characters and write a dialogue between this character and a favorite character from a Newbery award-winning book.

5. Select a favorite modern-day children's book and a favorite classic. Imagine that the character in the modern-day book took a quantum leap and found himself/herself in the pages of the classic. Write a brief journal entry that expresses the difference he/she has found.

6. Involve students in a discussion of "What is a classic?" What modern-day books do they think will become tomorrow's classics?

7. Have students create *Something About the Author—the Classics,* a book similar to the one they created in General Activity 5 on page 118.

8. Many classics were transformed into "Classic Comics." In groups, have students choose a favorite classic and create their own comic book that retells the story. (Share various comic books with students so that they have an understanding of the components of a comic book.)

Award-Winning Literature

In addition to the Newbery Medal and the Caldecott Medal, many other awards are given each year for outstanding children's literature. The list below represents several of these awards:

1. *The Laura Ingalls Wilder Award*: Given every three years to an author or illustrator whose books, published in the United States, have made a significant and lasting contribution to the literature of children. (Until 1980, the award was given out once every five years.)

2. *The Scott O'Dell Award for Historical Fiction*: Awarded annually to a book of historical fiction for children that has unusual literary merit. Established by O'Dell in 1981, the recipient must be a U.S. citizen and the book must have been published by a U.S. publisher.

3. *The International Reading Association Children's Award*: Given annually to an author who shows universal promise in the field of children's literature.

4. *Coretta Scott King Award*: Given annually to an author for outstanding literature that promotes multicultural understanding. In 1979, the award also recognized illustrators.

The Laura Ingalls Wilder Award

1954   Laura Ingalls Wilder

1960   Clara Ingram Judson

1965   Ruth Sawyer

1970   E.B. White

1975   Beverly Cleary

1980   Theodore Geisel (Dr. Seuss)

1983   Maurice Sendak

1986   Jean Fritz

1989   Elizabeth George Speare

1992   Marcia Brown

1995   Virginia Hamilton

The Scott O'Dell Award for Historical Fiction

1984   *The Sign of the Beaver*—Elizabeth George Speare

1985   *The Fighting Ground*—Avi

1986   *Sarah, Plain and Tall*—Patricia MacLachlan

1987   *Streams to the River, River to the Sea: A Novel of Sacagawea*—Scott O'Dell

1988   *Charley Skedaddle*—Patricia Beatty

1989   *The Honorable Prison*—Lyll Becerra de Jenkins

1990   *Shades of Gray*—Carolyn Reeder

1991   *Time of Troubles*—Pieter Van Raven

1992   *Stepping on the Cracks*—Mary D. Hahn

International Reading Association Children's Book Award

1975   *Transport 7-41-R* by T. Degens, Viking

1976   *Dragonwings* by Laurence Yep, Harper

1977   *A String in the Harp* by Nancy Bond, McElderry/Atheneum

1978   *A Summer to Die* by Lois Lowry, Houghton

1979   *Reserved for Mark Anthony Crowder* by Alison Smith, Dutton

1980   *Words by Heart* by Ouida Sebestyen, Atlantic/Little

1981   *My Own Private Sky* by Delores Beckman, Dutton

1982   *Good Night, Mr. Tom* by Michelle Magorian, Kestrel/Penguin (Great Britain); Harper (U.S.A.)

1983   *The Darkangel* by Meredith Ann Pierce, Atlantic/Little

1984   *Ratha's Creature* by Clare Bell, Atheneum

1985   *Badger on the Barger* by Janni Howker, McCray

1986   *Second Novel Prairie Songs* by Pam Conrad, Harper & Row

1987   Children's Book: *The Line Up Book* by Marisabini Russo, Greenwillow

        Young Adult: *After the Dancing Days* by Margaret I. Rostkowski, Harper & Row

1988   Children's Book: *The Third-Story Cat* by Leslie Baker, Little, Brown

        Young Adult: *The Ruby and the Smoke* by Philip Pullman, Random House

1989   Children's Book: *Rechenka's Eggs* by Patricia Polaccko, Putnam

        Young Adult: *Probably Still Nick* by Virginia Euwer Wolff, Holt

1990   Children's Book: *No Star Nights* by Anna Egan Smith and Steven Johnson, Random House

        Young Adult: *Children of the River* by Linda Crew, Delacorte Press

1991   Children's Book: *Is This a House for Hermit Crab?* by Megan McDonald and S.D. Schindler (illustrator), Orchard Books

        Young Adult: *Under the Hawthorn Tree* by Marita Conlon-McKenna, O'Brien Press, Dublin, Ireland, Holiday House

1992   Children's Book: *Ten Little Rabbits* by Virginia Grossman and Sylvia Long (illustrator), Chronicle Books

        Young Adult: *Rescue Josh McGuire* by Ben Mikaelsen, Hyperion Books

1993   Children's Book: *Old Turtle* by Douglas Wood and Cheng-Khee Chee (illustrator), Pfeiffer-Hamilton Publishers

        Young Adult: *Letters from Rifka* by Karen Hesse, Henry Holt and Company

1994 Younger Children: *Sweet Clara and the Freedom Quilt,* by Deborah H. Hopkins

Older Children: *Behind the Secret Window,* by Nellie Toll

1995 Younger Children: *The Ledger Book of Thomas Blue Eagle* by G. Matthaei, J. Grutman, & A. Cvijanovic, Thomasson-Grant, Inc.

Older Children: *Spite Fences* by T. Krisher, Bantam Books

Informational Readers: *Stranded at Plimoth Plantation 1626* by G. Bowen, HarperCollins

Coretta Scott King Awards

1970 *Martin Luther King, Jr.: Man of Peace* by Lillie Patterson, Garrard

1971 *Black Troubador: Langston Hughes* by Charlemae Rollins, Rand

1972 *17 Black Artists* by Elton C. Fax, Dodd

1973 *I Never Had It Made* by Jackie Robinson as told to Alfred Duckett, Putnam

1974 Author: *Ray Charles* by Sharon Bell Mathis, Crowell

Illustrator: The same title, illustrated by George Ford

1975 Author: *The Legend of Africana* by Dorothy Robinson, Johnson

Illustrator: The same title, illustrated by Herbert Temple

1976 Author: *Duey's Tale* by Pearl Bailey, Harcourt

Illustrator: No award

1977 Author: *The Story of Stevie Wonder* by James Haskins, Lothrop

Illustrator: No award

1978 Author: *Africa Dream* by Eloise Greenfield, Day/Crowell

Illustrator: The same title, illustrated by Carole Bayard

1979 Author: *Escape to Freedom* by Ossie Davis, Viking

Illustrator: *Something on My Mind* by Nikki Grimes, illustrated by Tom Feelings, Dial

1980 Author: *The Young Landlords* by Walter Dean Myers, Viking

Illustrator: *Cornrows* by Camille Yarbrough, illustrated by Carole Bayard, Coward

1981 Author: *This Life* by Sidney Poitier, Knopf

Illustrator: *Beat the Story-Drum, Pum-Pum* by Ashley Bryan, Atheneum

1982 Author: *Let the Circle Be Unbroken* by Mildred Taylor, Dial

Illustrator: *Mother Crocodile: An Uncle Amadou Tale from Senegal* adapted by Rosa Guy, illustrated by John Steptoe, Delacorte

1983 Author: *Sweet Whispers, Brother Rush* by Virginia Hamilton, Philomel

Illustrator: *Black Child* by Peter Mugabane, Knopf

1984 Author: *Everett Anderson's Good-Bye* by Lucille Clifton, Holt

Illustrator: *My Mama Needs Me* by Mildred Pitts Walter, illustrated by Pat Cummings, Lothrop

1985 Author: *Motown and Didi* by Walter Dean Myers, Viking

Illustrator: No award

1986   Author: *The People Could Fly: American Black Folktales* by Virginia Hamilton, Knopf

Illustrator: *Patchwork Quilt* by Valerie Flournoy, illustrated by Jerry Pinkney

1987   Author: *Justin and the Best Biscuits in the World* by Mildred Pitts Walter, Lothrop

Illustrator: *Half Moon and One Whole Star* by Crescent Dragonwagon, illustrated by Jerry Pinkney, Macmillan

1988   Author: *The Friendship* by Mildred D. Taylor, illustrated by Max Ginsburg, Dial

Illustrator: *Mufaro's Beautiful Daughters: An African Tale* retold and illustrated by John Steptoe, Lothrop

1989   Author: *Fallen Angels* by Walter Dean Myers, Scholastic

Illustrator: *Mirandy and Brother Wind* by Patricia McKissack, illustrated by Jerry Pinkney, Knopf

1990   Author: *A Long Hard Journey* by Patricia and Frederick McKissack, Walker

Illustrator: *Nathaniel Talking* by Eloise Greenfield, illustrated by Jan Spivey Gilchrist, Black Butterfly Press

1991   Author: *Road to Memphis* by Mildred D. Taylor, Dial

Illustrator: *Aida* retold by Leontyne Price, illustrated by Leo and Diane Dillon, Harcourt

1992   Author: *Now Is Your Time! The African-American Struggle for Freedom* by Walter Dean Myers, HarperCollins

Illustrator: *Tar Beach* by Faith Ringgold, Crown

1993   Author: *The Dark Thirty Southern Tales of the Supernatural* by Patricia McKissack, Knopf

Illustrator: *The Origin of Life on Earth: An African Creation Myth* by David A. Anderson, illustrated by Kathleen Atkins Wilson, Sights Productions

1994   Author: *Toning the Sweep*, by Angela Johnson, Orchard

Illustrator: "Soul Looks Back in Wonder," by Tom Feeling, *A Collection of African American Poets*, Editor: Phyllis Fogelman, Dial

1995   Author: *Christmas in the Big House, Christmas in the Quarters*, by Patricia and Frederick McKissack, Scholastic

Illustrator: *The Creation*, by James E. Ransome, poem by James Weldon Johnson, Holiday House

Activities

1. Have students create a traveling book mobile that features the award winners of a specific award for children's literature or books of an award-winning children's book author. Have them decorate the book mobile with book jackets, author pictures, and the name of the award being highlighted.

2. Involve students in reading book reviews of children's literature. Select a specific award and have students each select one of the award-winning books. Involve them in writing a review modeled after the reviews read. Encourage them to include their opinions as to whether or not the book should have been so honored. Create a monthly class "Book Review" publication and select several reviews to appear in it each month.

3. Group students—each group focusing on a different award. Have students in each group select one of the books that has won that award. Have them read the book and cooperatively create a mini-unit in which they create questions and activities based upon the book. Have groups share their units and become involved in one or more of the units developed by other groups.

4. Have students create a new award, giving it a name and a purpose. Students can suggest designs for the award, voting on the one they like best. Have students nominate books they have read that year by filling in a nomination form that has also been designed by the class. Display the nomination forms, encouraging students to read the books nominated. Conduct an election in which students vote for the book of their choice. Hold an awards ceremony and display the award-winning books and runner-ups.

Censorship and Children's Literature

In recent years, more and more pressure has been exerted by individuals and groups seeking to influence the content of children's literature. Those who wish to control children's reading choices find the issues, ideas, and language of many books inappropriate for children. Those who oppose censorship of literature are concerned with the principle of intellectual freedom. Below are many popular award-winning books that have been banned for the reasons listed next to the titles. The activities will involve students in becoming aware of the causes and effects of censorship and the way our country works to defend individual rights.

References

Blume, J. (1970). *Are you there, God? It's me, Margaret.* New York: Bradbury. [Challenged because protagonist is allowed to choose her own religion and because book discusses puberty.]

Blume, J. (1974). *Blubber.* New York: Bradbury.

[Challengers said that in the book bad behavior is never punished.]

Grimm, J. and Grimm, W. (1988). *Hansel and Gretel.* Illustrated by A. Browne. New York: Knopf.

[Challenged because it teaches children that it is acceptable to kill witches and depicts witches as child-eating monsters.]

Grimm, J. and Grimm, W. (1974). *Snow White.* Illustrated by T.S. Hyman. Boston: Little, Brown.

[Challenged because of its graphic violence; a hunter kills a wild boar, a wicked witch orders Snow White's heart to be torn out.]

Lowry, L . (1979). *Anastasia Krupkik.* Boston: Houghton.

[Challenged because of its language and the book's occasional reference to underage drinking.]

Maruki, T. (1982). *Hiroshima no pika.* New York: Lothrop, Lee and Shepard.

[Challenged because it shows the devastating effects of war and leaves the reader feeling that war is far from a noble endeavor.]

Paterson, K. (1977). *Bridge to Terabithia.* New York: Crowell.

[Challenged because of its language and reference to witchcraft.]

Paterson, K. (1978). *The Great Gilly Hopkins.* New York: Crowell.

[Challenged because of its language.]

Sendak, M. (1970). *In the Night Kitchen*. New York: Harper.

[Challenged because it "could lay the foundation for future use of pornography."]

Shyer, M. (1978). *Welcome home, Jellybean*. New York: Scribner.

[Challenged because two school board members considered the book depressing.]

Silverstein, S. (1981). *A light in the attic*. New York: Harper.

[Challenged because one of the poems is illustrated with a caricature of a person whose nude behind has been stung by a bee; challenged because the poem "Little Abigail and the Beautiful Pony" is morbid.]

Silverstein, S. (1964). *The giving tree*. New York: Harper.

[Challenge by feminists as condoning sexist stereotypes.]

Slepian, J. (1980). *The Alfred summer*. New York: Macmillan.

[Challenged because of language.]

Taylor, T. (1989). *The cay*. New York: Doubleday.

[Challenged because it allegedly maligns African-Americans.]

Twain, M. (1989). *Adventures of Tom Sawyer*. Illustrated by B. Moser. New York: Morrow. (1876)

[Challenged because of its inclusion of a degrading, offensive slang word to describe a black person.]

Yep, L. (1977). *Dragonwings*. New York: Harper.

[Challenged because of the frequent use of the word "demon" in the book and the belief by some that it might encourage children to commit suicide because they think they can be reincarnated as something or someone else.]

Activities

1. Discuss the term *censorship* with students. Try to obtain a group consensus of the definition.

2. Provide students with copies of the Bill of Rights. Have them write and deliver a persuasive speech to reflect their interpretation of the First Amendment as it applies to censorship of children's literature.

3. Survey students to discover which of the banned books listed in the references above they have read. Select one of the books that a majority of students have read or are familiar with and have students prepare a mock trial in which the book itself is tried for the reason(s) cited by those who challenged it.

4. Have students look at censorship in a different way by completing the following analogies. Once they have completed the analogies, have them draw their own interpretive illustration of censorship by combining their responses in a creative way.

   Censorship is like (name of a vegetable) because _____.

   Censorship is like (name of an animal) because _____.

   Censorship is like (name of a country) because _____.

   Censorship is like (name of a mineral) because _____.

5. Invite speakers from organizations such as The American Civil Liberties Union to speak to the class or call the American Library Association, Office for Intellectual Freedom (312-280-4223), for more information on censorship of children's books.

6. In 1992, 600 incidents of attempted censorship were reported to the American Library Association. This, however, is only a fraction of the actual attempts. Have students respond to the following question by creating a one-frame comic strip: "What if all books that were challenged were actually banned . . . "

7. The American Library Association's Office for Intellectual Freedom is the only library censorship monitoring group. Each year, for one week in September, the American Library Association sponsors a "Banned Books Week . . . Celebrating the Freedom to Read." Have students plan and take part in a week of activities that brings attention to the issues relating to censorship.

8. Involve students in a discussion of the following questions:

   a. What types of censorship exist? (moral, military, political, religious, etc.)

   b. How does censorship affect your life?

   c. Why do some people feel censorship is important?

   d. Why do some people feel that censorship is never justified?

   e. Should book censorship be allowed? If so, in what situations?

   f. If book censorship were allowed, who should determine what is and what is not censored?

Intermediate Unit: Fractions

Theme: FRACTIONS

Focus: Students will learn how fractions are an important part of our daily lives.

Objectives: On completion of this thematic unit, students will be able to:

1. Understand the value of fractions in the everyday world.
2. Describe various ways of using fractions.
3. Demonstrate the use of fractions in different situations.
4. Be able to use fractions correctly.

Initiating Activity: Invite students to list all the different ways in which fractions are used in everyday life—for example, in cooking, in weather predictions, in sports scores, and so on. Ask students to create a large wall mural of the various activities and occupations that use fractions on a regular basis. Students may wish to interview other students, parents, or adults about some of the ways in which fractions are used in their lives. Additional ideas or situations can be added to the wall mural throughout the year.

General Activities:

1. Provide students with one or more copies of selected cookbooks (see the bibliographies). Ask students to record several recipes and to note the various ways in which fractions are used. If possible, provide opportunities for students to prepare some of the recipes to share with each other.

2. Invite students to talk about various ways in which fractions are used in different sports (for example, the first half, the last quarter, a quarter-mile race, and so on). Which sport uses fractions the most? Which sports do not use any fractions?

3. Ask students to look through the daily newspaper and note the instances in which fractions are used to report significant news events (for example, "After a $2\frac{1}{2}$-mile chase through city streets, the police were only able to recover $\frac{1}{3}$ of the bank money"). Invite students to maintain an ongoing news journal of fraction uses.

4. Invite a mathematician from a local college or university to visit your classroom. Ask that person to discuss the different ways in which fractions are used in everyday life. Have students prepare a list of questions before the visit.

5. Invite students to prepare the following recipe for brownies. Later, challenge them to compute the amount of ingredients for (a) twice as many people, and (b) half as many people:

   3 ounces unsweetened chocolate

   6 tablespoons butter

   1 cup sugar

   3 eggs

1½ teaspoons vanilla extract

½ cup cake flour

¼ teaspoon baking soda

¾ cup walnut halves

½ cup chocolate chips

Preheat oven to 325 degrees. Melt the chocolate and butter over low heat, stirring constantly. Remove from the heat and pour into a large mixing bowl. Beat in the sugar. Add eggs, one at a time, beating well after each addition. Stir in vanilla. Fold in flour and baking soda. Pour the batter into a well-greased 8 x 8 inch pan. Sprinkle with nuts and chocolate chips. Bake 25 minutes. Cool one hour before slicing.

6. Invite the music teacher to demonstrate to students how fractions are used to write music. Ask him or her to explain ½ notes, ¼ notes, and ⅛ notes. Help students understand that each musical note is a fraction of the whole.

7. Have students work to create a "Fraction Concentration Game." On one card write a fraction (such as "½") and on an opposing card its equivalent (for example, "⅛"). Create a pack of 20 to 25 pairs and invite students to play the game with each other.

8. Challenge students to look in textbooks other than their math book for examples of fractions. How are fractions used in their social studies or science texts, for example?

Discussion Questions:

1. Why is it important for people to know about fractions? (Answers will vary.)

2. How are fractions used in everyday life? Do adults use fractions more than kids? If so, why? (Answers will vary.)

3. What are some of the ways in which fractions are used around your home? On what types of items or objects would you most likely find fractions? (Answers will vary.)

4. If you could be any fraction, which one would you be? Why? (Answers will vary.)

Literature Related Activities

Title:	*If You Made a Million*
Genre:	Picture Book
Author:	David M. Schwartz
Bibliographic Information:	Lothrop, Lee & Shepard, New York, 1989
Summary:	Various monetary values are presented in this intriguing tale of a marvelous magician and the ways in which he explains the concept of equivalence.
Interest Level:	Grades 3–6.

1. Pre-Reading Activity:

    Ask students to compute the various combinations of coins that will equal $1.00. Can students combine four coins to equal $1.00? Five coins? Seven coins? More than ten coins? Invite students to illustrate the various possible coin combinations that equal $1.00. These can be displayed on a large wall chart.

2. Learning Activities:

    a. The author states that $1 million is equivalent to a 360-foot pile of one dollar bills. Ask students to determine the height of $200,000, $50,000, or $150,000. Do they know of any objects that might be equivalent to the height of $1 million?

    b. Invite students to divide the $1 million into five piles. How much money would be in each pile? How much money would be in each of 20 piles? How much in each of 50 piles?

    c. Invite students to investigate the average weight of a whale. What objects weigh half as much as a whale? What objects weigh one-tenth as much as a whale? One twentieth as much as a whale?

    d. How much money would each person in the class get if the $1 million was divided equally (including the teacher!).

3. Discussion Questions:

    a. How much would each person in your family get if that money was divided equally among all family members? (Answers will vary.)

    b. What would you do with $1 million? (Answers will vary.)

    c. What made this an interesting (or uninteresting) book? (Answers will vary.)

    d. What are some of the ways in which fractions could have been used by the author, but were not? (Answers will vary.)

Title:	*Fractions Are Parts of Things*
Genre:	Nonfiction
Author:	J. Richard Dennis
Bibliographic Information:	Crowell, New York, 1971
Summary:	A variety of illustrations and hands-on activities provide readers with a thorough introduction to fractions and their uses.
Interest Level:	Grades 2–6.

---

1. Pre-Reading Activity:

    Invite students to look around the classroom and locate items that have been divided into fractions (for example, the blackboard may be in two equal sections, someone's chocolate bar may be divided into eight equal sections). Have students create an ongoing poster of the items that are divided into fractions. Be sure to share with students the idea that fractions are equal parts of a whole object (each part within the object must be of equal size in order for them to qualify as fractions).

2. Learning Activities:

   a. Ask the class to brainstorm for various ways in which they can divide themselves into different categories of fractions. For example, students with blue eyes and students with brown eyes; students with blond hair, red hair, brunette hair; students in various age categories (by years or by total months). Have students chart their discoveries on a large mural.

   b. Ask students to experiment with Cuisenaire rods and the fractions that can result from their use. For example, ten white pieces is equivalent to one orange rod, thus one white piece can be represented by the fraction ⅒. Invite students to create equivalents of other selected fractions.

   c. Ask students to experiment with the fractional shapes on page 8 of the book. How can they determine whether the white pieces are equivalent to the black pieces and vice versa? How can they demonstrate those relationships?

   d. Some of the most "widely used" fractions are ½, ⅓, ¼, and ¾. Ask students to locate examples of those fractions throughout the classroom and throughout their homes. Which fraction is used the most?

3. Discussion Questions:

   a. How would you rewrite this book for someone who did not speak English? (Answers will vary.)

   b. What made this an easy book to understand? (Answers will vary.)

   c. What are some of the ways in which your parents use fractions in the kitchen? In the living room? In the garage? (Answers will vary.)

   d. How many ways have you used fractions to describe events in your own life? (Answers will vary.)

Title: *The Magic School Bus at the Waterworks*

Genre: Picture Book

Author: Joanna Cole

Bibliographic Information: Scholastic, New York, 1986

Summary: Ms. Frizzle and her class take a most unusual trip to the waterworks, where they are turned into a drop of water and eventually wind up coming out of a faucet.

Interest Level: Grades 3-6.

1. Pre-Reading Activity:

   Invite students to collect different measuring devises that will measure quantities of water. How many different types of measuring cups, vessels, or containers can students locate? Indicate to students that most of these instruments indicate various portions of water—each of which is a fraction of a larger quantity (16 ounces = 1 cup; 2 pints = 1 quart; and so on.). Invite students to draw various illustrations of these measuring tools.

2. Learning Activities:

   a. Invite students to measure the size of a raindrop (or the amount of water in a single raindrop). How many raindrops would it take to equal one ounce; to equal one cup; to equal one quart?

   b. Ask students to measure the amount of water lost because a single faucet is dripping (perhaps a faucet in the classroom). How much water is lost in a day, in a week, in a year?

   c. The book indicates that approximately two-thirds of a human being's body is composed of water. Invite students to calculate how much water that would be for the average-sized child and/or the average-sized adult.

   d. Have students place various (equal-shaped) containers of water in the open sun and calculate the amount of time necessary for the water in each to completely evaporate.

3. Discussion Questions:

   a. What would make Ms. Frizzle an interesting teacher to have for this classroom? (Answers will vary.)

   b. What might be some of the sights a raindrop evaporating over this school might see as it ascends into the sky? (Answers will vary.)

   c. What did you enjoy most about this book? Would you enjoy reading other books in the series? (Answers will vary.)

   d. What are some ways in which students can help to conserve water? (repair leaky faucets, use less water, and so on.)

Title:	*Gator Pie*
Genre:	Picture Book
Author:	Louise Mathews
Bibliographic Information:	Dodd, Mead, New York, 1979
Summary:	Two alligators discover a pie and are about to eat it when several other alligators want equal pieces. A disagreement ensues, but all is well as Alice and Alvin are able to get everything they want.
Interest Level:	Grades 3–6.

1. Pre-Reading Activity:

   Bring in an inexpensive pie from the frozen food section of your local grocery market. Invite students to determine how the pie could be cut so that each member of the class would get an equal-sized piece. What would happen if two people in the class decided that they didn't want a piece of pie? What would happen if two additional people joined the class? Invite students to illustrate their responses.

2. Learning Activities:

   a. Invite students to each make up the following recipe for "Peanut Butter Play Dough":

      1 cup of peanut butter

      $1\frac{1}{4}$ cup sugar

      1 cup corn syrup

      $1\frac{1}{2}$ cup dry milk

      Mix all the ingredients until well blended (add more dry milk if mixture is too sticky).

      Have students spread their mixtures into individual pie plates. Invite them to evenly divide the "pies" into various fractions to serve eight, ten, fourteen, twenty, and/or twenty-five people. What difficulties do they note?

   b. Invite students to collect recipes from home in which fractions are used. Have students discuss the importance of accurate measurements in the preparation of selected recipes.

   c. Invite students to divide a classroom object, such as a table or desk, into various fractions. Have students divide the object into equal sections using lengths of masking tape. How is this division process similar to or different from the division of a circular object such as a pie?

   d. In the book, the pie must be cut into 100 equal pieces. Invite students to discuss various ways in which this might be done. What difficulties are encountered when a pie must be divided into many pieces?

3. Discussion Questions:

   a. Aside from food items, what are some other things that sometimes must be divided into equal pieces? (lumber, water pipes, and so on)

   b. What did you enjoy most about this book? What did you enjoy least? (Answers will vary.)

   c. Does everything shared between two friends always have to "be equal"? (Answers will vary.)

   d. What kinds of things do you enjoy sharing with your friends? (Answers will vary.)

Culminator: The culminating activity could be a "Fraction Day." Challenge students to use only fractions throughout an entire day. Instead of saying or writing a whole number (14, for example), encourage students to use the fractional representation of that number ($\frac{28}{2}$, for example). Invite students to use fractions in stories they write, conversations they have with each other, and other classroom events in which numbers are used. At the end of the day, discuss with students some of the challenges they faced in converting all the numbers into fractions.

Supplemental Literature

Primary (Grades 1–3):

Hoban, L. (1981). *Arthur's funny money*. New York: Harper and Row.

This is the story of how Arthur goes about earning enough money to buy a favorite T-shirt.

Howe, J. (1990). *Harold and Chester in hot fudge*. New York: Morrow.

Four pets are embroiled in a mystery about some fudge and its chocolate covering.

Hutchins, P. (1986). *The doorbell rang*. New York: Greenwillow.

Two children discover how a batch of cookies can be divided into several different fractions.

Lionni, L. (1975). *Pezzattino*. New York: Pantheon.

The concepts of fractions (from the perspective of a square) is invitingly told in this tale of discovery and adventure.

Maestro, B. and Maestro, G. (1988). *Dollars and cents for Harriet*. New York: Crown.

The story illustrates some of the clever ways an elephant earns enough money to purchase a cherished toy.

McNamera, L. (1972). *Henry's pennies*. New York: Franklin Watts.

This is the story of a boy who collects pennies, nothing but pennies, and how he uses his earnings to purchase a special pet.

Pomerantz, C. (1984). *The half-birthday party*. New York: Clarion.

The fraction ½ is the centerpiece of this story about a birthday party and things that are divided in half.

Intermediate (Grades 4–6):

Adams, L. and Coudert, A. (1983). *Alice and the boa constrictor*. Boston: Houghton Mifflin.

Alice has some creative ideas for raising the money she needs to purchase a boa constrictor.

Conford, E. (1989). *What's cooking, Jenny Archer?* Boston: Little, Brown.

Jenny learns (the hard way) about making money and all the expenses that go along with any business enterprise.

Kleven, J. (1982). *The Turtle Street Trading Co.* New York: Delacorte Press.

Four friends learn all the ins and outs of any business enterprise as they work toward a treasured goal.

Levitin, S. (1974). *Jason and the money tree*. New York: Harcourt Brace Jovanovich.

Jason plants some money in his back yard and is amazed to discover the results—not only in terms of what grows, but the implications.

Silverstein, S. (1964). *A Giraffe and a half*. New York: Harper and Row.

An engaging and delightful story that helps readers imagine and fantasize about one particular fraction.

Watson, C. (1972). *Tom Fox and the apple pie*. New York: Crowell.

The story of a fox, a pie, and the various ways in which that pie can be divided is marvelously told in this tale of imagination and reality.

MINI-THEMES

Decimals

Decimals are just another way of expressing fractions. We use decimals in many aspects of our lives, and youngsters are often surprised to discover that many of the measurements they take for granted are actually decimals. The following collection of books would all be wonderful additions to the math library of any classroom.

References

Anno, M. (1984). *Anno's flea market.* New York: Philomel Books.

Brenner, B. (1989). *Annie's pet.* New York: Bantam Books.

Butterworth, N. and Inkpen, M. (1989). *Just like Jasper!* Boston: Little, Brown.

Caple, K. (1986). *The purse.* Boston: Houghton Mifflin.

Conford, E. (1988). *A job for Jennie Archer.* Boston: Little, Brown.

Day, A. (1989). *Paddy's pay-day.* New York: Viking.

Heide, F. (1981). *Treehorn's treasures.* New York: Holiday House.

Kotzwinkle, W. (1970). *The day the gang got rich.* New York: Viking.

Shaw, N. (1991). *Sheep in a shop.* Boston: Houghton Mifflin.

Van Leeuwen, J. (1983). *Benjy in business.* New York: Dutton.

Activities

1. Invite students to investigate the various ways in which decimals are used in everyday transactions. Aside from money, what are some other instances in which decimals are utilized? In which sports are decimals used?

2. Invite students to take individual walking "field trips" throughout the local community, locating different signs and billboards on which there are one or more decimals. How are those decimals represented? Why were decimals used instead of fractions?

3. Have students look through an edition of the local newspaper for examples of decimals. In what section would you expect to discover the most decimals? In what section would you find the least?

4. Ask students to select one of the previously mentioned books on fractions. Challenge students to convert all the fractions in the book(s) to decimals. Were there some fractions that could not be converted? What difficulties were encountered?

Cooking and Eating

Kids love to cook! Cooking is one of the most enjoyable learning activities teachers and children can share together. Cooking can not only be used as a forum for studying fractions and decimals, but can also be used to illustrate proper nutritional habits, science concepts, social customs, and a host of other significant events in all curricular areas.

References

Blain, D. (1991). *The boxcar children cookbook*. Morton Grove, IL: Albert Whitman.

Cresswell, H. (1968). *The piemakers*. New York: Lippincott.

Douglass, B. (1985). *The chocolate chip cookie contest*. New York: Lothrop, Lee & Shepard.

Khalsa, D. (1989). *How pizza came to Queens*. New York: Potter.

Levitin, S. (1980). *Nobody stole the pie*. New York: Harcourt Brace Jovanovich.

MacDonald, K. (1985). *The Anne of Green Gables cookbook*. Toronto: Oxford University Press.

MacGregor, C. (1967). *The storybook cookbook*. Garden City, NY: Doubleday.

McMillan, B. (1991). *Eating fractions*. New York: Scholastic.

Watson, N. (1987). *The little pig's first cookbook*. Boston: Little, Brown.

Wellington, A. (1978). *Apple pie*. Englewood Cliffs, NJ: Prentice-Hall.

Willard, N. (1990). *The high rise glorious skittle skat roarious sky pie angel food cake*. New York: Harcourt Brace Jovanovich.

Activities

1. Ask students to prepare one or more of the recipes in the recipe books above. Invite them to "customize" a selected recipe in terms of the number of people being fed. For example, what measurements (for a cake, pie, or cookie recipe) would have to be used to give everyone in the class an equal portion?

2. Here is a recipe for "Peanut Butter Pie" that students will enjoy:

    > 1 8-ounce package of cream cheese
    >
    > 1 cup of confectioner's sugar
    >
    > 1 cup of peanut butter
    >
    > ½ cup of milk
    >
    > 1 13-ounce package of Cool Whip®
    >
    > 2 prepared graham cracker crusts

    Mix the first four ingredients and then fold in the Cool Whip®. Spread the mixture into the graham cracker crusts.

    After students have prepared their pies, have them divide the pies into various fractions and photograph them for presentation in a large "Fraction Notebook." Afterwards, the pies can be eaten.

3. Ask students to bring in different examples of measuring cups and utensils. What similarities are observed? What significant differences? Discuss with students the importance of accurate measurement during cooking.

4. The following recipe for "Incredible Edible Cookies" makes about 12 dozen cookies. Ask students to rewrite the recipe to serve different groups of people (for example, four dozen people, 36 people, 24 people). Ask students to reduce one of the ingredients (for example, if the

chocolate chips were reduced to two ounces, how much would each of the other ingredients need to be reduced?).

>   1 cup margarine, softened
>
>   2 cups peanut butter
>
>   2 cups sugar
>
>   1 pound brown sugar
>
>   6 eggs
>
>   dash of light corn syrup
>
>   8 ounces chocolate chips
>
>   8 ounces M & M's®
>
>   4 teaspoons baking soda
>
>   1 teaspoon vanilla
>
>   ½ cup chopped nuts
>
>   1 cup raisins
>
>   9 cups uncooked quick oats

Preheat the oven to 350 degrees. Mix together all the ingredients in a *very* large bowl, adding the oats last. Drop by heaping teaspoons onto an ungreased cookie sheet. Bake for 10 to 12 minutes.

Money

Teaching students the value and uses of money is just as important as teaching them about the relationships between different denominations of coins and paper money. A wide selection of children's literature helps students understand the relationships that can and should exist between money and its uses.

References

Adler, D. (1985). *Inflation*. New York: Franklin Watts.

Adler, D. (1984). *Prices go up, prices go down*. New York: Franklin Watts.

Barkin, C. and James, E. (1990). *Jobs for kids*. New York: Lothrop, Lee & Shepard.

Dumbleton, M. (1991). *Dial-A-Croc*. New York: Orchard Books.

Houser, P. and Bradley, H. (1989). *How to teach children about money*. Denver, CO: Western Freelance Writing Services.

Marshall, J. (1986). *Yummers too*. Boston: Houghton Mifflin.

Martin, C. (1984). *Summer business*. New York: Greenwillow.

Scott, E. (1985). *Stocks and bonds, profits and losses*. New York: Franklin Watts.

Wilkinson, E. (1989). *Making cents: Every kid's guide to money*. Boston: Little, Brown.

Young, J. and Young, J. (1976). *The kids' money-making book*. Garden City, NY: Doubleday.

Activities

1. Discuss with students some of the ways in which people earn money. What are some of the ways in which students have traditionally earned spending money? Which ways are the most profitable?

2. Invite students to do some comparison shopping in their neighborhood or community. Provide student teams each with a list of six or seven specific grocery items. Ask each team to visit a variety of stores and record the prices for each of those items. Have students discuss reasons why there may be price differences between stores.

3. Provide each student with a different amount of money under a dollar (use play money or tokens). Challenge students to convert their money into fractions of a dollar (for example, 43 cents would be 43/100 of a dollar; 25 cents would be 1/4 of a dollar). What challenges do they encounter?

4. Invite the owner of a local coin shop to visit the classroom to discuss the different types of coinage displayed in the store. What types of American coins does he or she have that are different from those we currently use today? Have the individual discuss the reasons why some coins are more valuable than others.

Index

More Thematic Units

Index

Creating the Integrated Curriculum

About the Authors

LIZ ROTHLEIN, full professor, is an Associate Dean in the School of Education at the University of Miami. She is coauthor of more than 20 books about reading, language arts, environmental and multicultural issues, and of other popular resource books for using children's literature in elementary classrooms. She is the recipient of numerous teaching awards, including Professor of the year at the University of Miami, and is listed in Outstanding Elementary Teachers of America.

ANTHONY D. FREDERICKS is an Associate Professor of Education at York College, York, Pennsylvania where he teaches methods courses in reading and language arts. A former classroom teacher and reading specialist, he is a frequent presenter and storyteller at school assemblies, inservice workshops, and reading conferences throughout North America. He is the author or co-author of more than two dozen teacher resource books in a variety of curricular areas including the enormously popular *Frantic Frogs and Other Frankly Fractured Folktales for Readers Theatre*, the award-winning *Social Studies Through Children's Literature: An Integrated Approach*, and the best-selling series of books — *Involving Parents Through Children's Literature*.

ANITA MEYER MEINBACH has worked for the Dade County Public Schools as a classroom teacher, curriculum writer, and teacher trainer, providing seminars and guidance in curriculum development. As an adjunct professor at the University of Miami, she teaches courses in language arts, reading, and children's literature. Dr. Meinbach is the author of several textbooks and numerous resource books in reading and language arts. A frequent presenter at various workshops and professional conferences, she speaks on a variety of topics dealing with children's literature, the interdisciplinary approach to learning, and curriculum development.